CONNECTED WOMEN

Inspiring women who have shaped the world and each other

KATE HODGES

Foreword by
Lucy Mangan

WHITE LION
PUBLISHING

Contents

Foreword

I THINK of my grandma every time I'm doing laundry. After doing a load – by hand, then pushing it through the mangle, the whole olde worlde works – she would turn all her husband's socks the right way out, peg them out and then carefully pair them up and put them in his drawer when they were dry. And she would iron his underpants and put them away too.

My mother had a washing machine, trained my dad to take his socks off so they stayed the right way out and didn't iron his underpants, but in all other respects the process remained the same.

I do my husband's laundry but his socks stay however he left them and if he wants them paired or his boxers flattened, he can (and does not) do it himself.

It is this tiny personal connection to past distaff generations of mine that reminds me – at least once a fortnight (I am always behind on laundry. Because I have a full-time job and a child too) – in a tiny personal way what progress women have made and how much more there is left to do.

Connections are important. Sometimes they constrain and undermine us, sometimes they support and liberate us. 'No man is an island,' wrote John Donne, meaning that no-one can survive, let alone thrive, alone.

And yet that is precisely what women have had to try and do throughout history, at least compared to men. Men have always been connected. They have always been out and about, meeting people in public and professional as well as private life. Their stories, their thoughts, their theories, their achievements, their progenitors, their idols, their teachers, their inspirations have always been lauded, logged and learned by all.

Women have traditionally moved in smaller spheres. Their stories, thoughts, achievements and much else have far less often been deemed worthy of recording in the annals of history. And the effect of this has been to isolate us – gently but effectively – from our contemporaries and from our forebears. Betty Friedan's identification of 'the problem that has no name' is emblematic of something that has been repeated in some form since time immemorial; she described the unspoken (often Valium-numbed) baffled despair of women sitting alone in their well-appointed marital homes wondering why they still felt so dissatisfied and despairing of the lives they had been told would meet their every need. *The Feminine Mystique* became a bestseller, and an enduring classic, because it connected all those women and has kept connecting them ever since. In the 70s women met in groups to engage in what was then called 'consciousness raising' – to make women aware of all that they had in common and the common enemies they had. The most modern and perhaps even more powerful counterpart has been Laura Bates' Everyday Sexism Project. It provided an online space – via Twitter – where women could record their experiences, large and small, of being harassed, assaulted, or treated in any one of a hundred million ways that made them feel humiliated, uncertain, anxious or in some way 'less than' the men around us.

The more connected we are, the more connected we make ourselves, within our own times and to our collective past, the less alone we feel. Individual experience becomes validated and it becomes a recognisable part of a recognisable pattern that cannot be ignored or dismissed by those who would otherwise be keen to do so. And once we are all aware of each other and the scale of the support that is out there, the more strength and force we can muster for action.

But it is as important to connect to our collective past as it is to forge bonds with our contemporaries. Because – aside from the simple unfairness visited on those whose achievements are stricken from the record – when women are written out of history, it deprives us not just of all the same things that we lose when we are isolated from contemporaries, but also dooms us to reinventing the wheel, time and time again. The first, second, third and fourth waves of feminism have all had to go far back over old ground before they could gain any new because the work of each predecessor had met with such concerted efforts to mock, marginalise and suppress. What energy has been lost over the years because we weren't told that this problem had been faced before, the solutions attempted, which failed and which succeeded?

The great thing now is that we live in an age where it is easier than ever to make your female voice heard. The internet has many – many, many, many – faults but we can still use it to join together in greater numbers online and (as the anti-Trump marches, Black Lives Matter and countless other campaigns show) in real life too. History is no longer written only by the victors. The record is not singular, homogenous or set in stone. Good luck trying to write the globally-famous and revered likes of Malala Yousafzai, Beyoncé, Oprah Winfrey or Michelle Obama out of history. It can no longer be done. Future generations will be able to stand on the shoulders of giants, just as men always have. Let's look forward, ladies, to taking in that glorious view and setting off towards it, scattering unwashed, unpaired socks in our wake.

Lucy Mangan, 2017

Introduction

BEHIND EVERY great woman is ... another great woman. In the pages of this book, you'll discover some incredible stories – tales of spies who smuggled secrets in their knickers, of glamorous film stars who had secret lives inventing the vital elements of Wi-Fi, of suffragettes who spent time in jail being force-fed, and of ex-slaves who led hundreds of others to freedom. You'll also find that these women rarely acted alone – they had the support of friends, cheerleaders and mentors, or were inspired by female groundbreakers who'd come before them.

The connections between these astonishing women are sometimes close – best friends, colleagues, lovers – or looser: they might share influences, have been part of the same movement, or won the same award. I've tried to avoid connections established through romantic relationships with men as far as I can – these stories are all about celebrating the sisterhood.

I've included some household names. You will already know Indira Gandhi, Eleanor Roosevelt and Queen Victoria, I'm sure, but you might not be aware of their connections: that a homesick Indira was comforted at her English boarding school by author Iris Murdoch, a strait-laced Eleanor Roosevelt went on wild flying trips dressed in ballgowns with Amelia Earhart, or that Queen Victoria

had a clandestine meeting with radical author Harriet Beecher Stowe.

There are other, more obscure, names – women who've lived incredible lives. It's an honour to bring to a little wider attention those whose stories are not as well known. I loved uncovering the tale of artist Claude Cahun, who blurred gender boundaries, played with conceptual art and narrowly escaped execution by the Nazis. Or Maeve Brennan, the hard-drinking, pin-sharp journalist who was immortalised as Holly Golightly in *Breakfast at Tiffany's*. Meanwhile, Kati Horna's quietly yet acutely observed portraits of women and children during the Spanish Civil War equal or surpass the flashier images of the same conflict taken on the battlefront by her lover Robert Capa.

We set some parameters: these women came into their prime from the nineteenth century onwards, and they obviously had to have at least some documented interaction with other women. I'd have loved to include Ching Shih the Chinese pirate, or Wanny Woldstad the Norwegian trapper, but their solitary lifestyles meant that connections with others were hard to find.

During my research, I found women whose accomplishments have been obliterated, or at the very least played down, by their colleagues or relatives. Fanny Mendelssohn might have been hailed as an important female composer far earlier had her brother not published her works under his name, and Lise Meitner might have won a Nobel Prize in Physics if her employer in Sweden had ignored her gender and appreciated her expertise.

Some entries were painful to write. Despite having read the story of Anne Frank countless times I still found it incredibly moving, and it was difficult to type through the tears. Others were eye-opening: the voracious and unapologetic sexual appetites of Mercedes de Acosta and Colette astonished me.

Sarah Papworth's vibrant and original illustrations are equal to the stories of these women; she brings each of them alive. Sarah's got an incredible talent for making a story sing from a page, and each of her pictures spins a representation not just of the woman you're reading about, but how she fitted into the world.

I worked to a soundtrack of the women's music. Nina Simone's performances still have the power to shift tectonic plates, Patti Smith remains an inspiration to artists around the world, and Mahalia Jackson's voice can raise your spirits from rock bottom to rafter-high in seconds. You'll find my Spotify playlist here: tiny.cc/connectedwomen.

The sisterhood is vast, and the concept of six degrees of separation spins the connections out far wider than a single book can contain. Sadly, yet inevitably, there wasn't space to include every woman I wanted. There wasn't enough room for Delia Derbyshire, Pussy Riot or Björk. No Vita Sackville-West, Toni Morrison or Elena Ferrante. No Beryl Burton, Tavi Gevinson, Vivian Maier or Patty Hearst. I missed Alexandrine Tinné, and couldn't squeeze in Marie Laveau or, to my great sadness, Lisa Simpson. However, the stories of the women I have included have astonished, inspired and thrilled me. I hope they do the same for you.

Kate Hodges, 2017

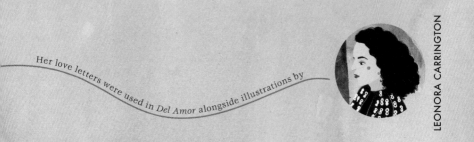

Her love letters were used in *Del Amor* alongside illustrations by

MANUELA SÁENZ lived a life that was a fierce blend of passionate love and political conviction. She was born illegitimately in Quito, Ecuador, but was fortunate that her father accepted her into his marital family. Manuela was provided for, educated in a convent and, after she was seduced by an army officer, 'protected' by an arranged marriage to a much older, wealthy English merchant, James Thorne, which was abhorrent but at least left her financially secure.

The two moved to Peru, where they lived an aristocratic lifestyle, hosting political leaders and military top brass. Manuela kept her ears open, soaking up secrets slipped from loose lips. Revolution was brewing, and she became radicalised, supporting the rebels who wanted freedom from Spain, the country that had colonised vast areas of South and Central America in the sixteenth century. Boldly, Manuela defied convention and left her husband to return to Quito.

It was there in 1822 that she met the love of her life, Simón Bolívar, or 'El Libertador', the revolutionary who freed much of South America from Spanish rule. The pair immediately connected on a passionate and political level. Manuela worked tirelessly as a spy, protested for women's rights, organised troops and helped nurse the injured. Loyal to Bolívar until the last, she even risked her own life to save him from assassination. In return, he dubbed her the 'Liberator of the Liberator'.

After an intense eight years together, Bolívar died from tuberculosis shortly before he was due to retire to Europe. Manuela was exiled and travelled to Jamaica and Peru. Despite an ignominious end to an exceptional, deeply unconventional life, Sáenz left a valuable legacy to South America. In 2010 her symbolic remains were removed from a communal grave in Paita, Peru, and interred alongside her soulmate in Caracas, Venezuala.

At the end of her life, Manuela scratched a living selling tobacco and translating letters for North American whale hunters (Herman Melville amongst them). During this time, the revolutionary Giuseppe Garibaldi journeyed to South America. Just like Manuela, he was mourning his own soulmate and political comrade-in-arms, Anita Garibaldi. The parallels in Manuela's and Giuseppe's lives would have made for an instant understanding and connection. Anita and Manuela's roles in shaping our current geopolitical landscape were initially overshadowed by the male figureheads, but the pair now stand for female emancipation across Latin America, and their role in the liberation of South America from Spanish rule cannot be overstated.

MANUELA SÁENZ

"libertadora del libertador"

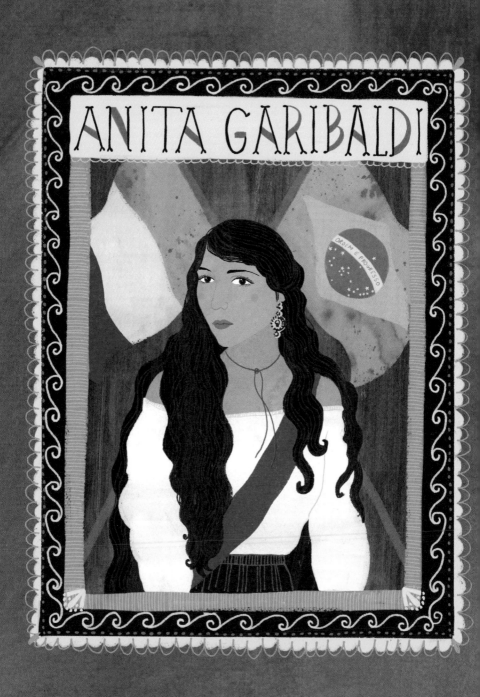

SOFIA KOVALEVSKAYA

ANNA JACLARD

LOUISE MICHEL

Took an active role in warfare, as did

ANOTHER GREAT love story rooted in the revolutionary political movements of the nineteenth century, Anita and Giuseppe Garibaldi fought shoulder to shoulder with South American and Italian rebel groups.

Anita was born in Brazil to a poor family of farmers and fishermen: a tough upbringing, but one that left her with outstanding horse riding skills and an inner grit. At fourteen, she was forced to marry, but shortly afterwards her husband abandoned her for the army.

In 1839, she met Giuseppe Garibaldi while he was fighting in a ten-year-long Republican uprising – the Ragamuffin War. He claimed his first words to her were the darkly romantic, if a little creepy, 'You must be mine.' Anita joined him on board his ship, the *Rio Pardo*, and from then on remained at his side.

Anita taught Giuseppe the art of horse riding, and about the gaucho lifestyle. They thundered into battle side by side, fighting with muskets, taking charge of munitions and nursing the wounded. During the Battle of Curitibanos in 1840, a pregnant Anita was separated from Giuseppe and captured, but escaped at a gallop on the back of a camp horse.

When the horse was shot, she leaped off, jumped into the river Canoas, then spent four days wandering without food in the woods. Eventually she was reunited with her love.

Being pregnant didn't slow Anita down a jot – at eight months she commanded the cavalry at the Battle of São José do Norte. She went on to have four children in total. Anita and Giuseppe moved to Montevideo in Uruguay, and eventually, in 1842, the couple married.

There was more war. The Garibaldis returned to Italy to fight against the Austrian Empire, a series of battles that ended in siege and illness. Pregnant and ill with malaria, Anita collapsed and died. Giuseppe was grief-stricken. Eleven years later he was still wearing Anita's striped scarf as he rode out to hail Victor Emmanuel II as king of a united Italy.

Anita's life combined intense romance with high adventure, and a big-screen adaptation of her story was inevitable. In 1952, directors Goffredo Alessandrini and Francesco Rosi directed Camicie rosse, which told her tale. The woman chosen to portray this tempestuous, brave firebrand was an actor known as 'la lupa', or the 'she-wolf' – Anna Magnani.

EXPRESSIVE, UNABASHED, and a breathtakingly skilled actress with a temper that frayed quickly, Anna Magnani was the 'volcanic earth mother of all Italian cinema'. Born of an Egyptian mother and an Italian father, Anna was raised in a poor area of Rome and educated at a French convent. It was while watching the nuns stage Christmas plays that she was inspired to act herself and, on leaving, she enrolled at drama school.

But it was on the flick-knife tough streets of the city that Anna was to really hone her acting chops. She'd run with gangs, and sing in nightclubs and cabaret joints to support herself. Anna wasn't your traditional film starlet beauty: her hair was wild and uncombed, her eyes lurked in shadows and she was stocky rather than willowy. However, those shadowed eyes were mesmerising, attitude oozed from every finger jab and heel turn, and her sexual magnetism spilled out from the screen.

In 1933, she married Goffredo Alessandrini, who cast her in *La cieca di Sorrento*. Anna took smaller roles to devote more time to her marriage, but left Goffredo seven years later. After a brief affair, she gave birth to a boy, Luca, who lost the use of his legs after a bout of polio. Anna resolved to earn enough to 'shield him forever from want'.

In 1945, Anna met Roberto Rossellini, with whom she had a tempestuous working and sexual relationship. Anna once said, 'Women like me can only submit to men capable of dominating them, and I have never found anyone

capable of dominating me.' Although Rossellini tried, after breaking half the crockery in Italy over each other's heads, the two split.

In 1951, Anna's masterful performance in Bellissima catapulted her to stardom. Work with some of the most talented directors in the world followed. Writer Tennessee Williams created *The Rose Tattoo* with her specifically in mind for the role of Serafina, for which she won an Oscar.

Anna Magnani's world-weary voice and her genuine empathy with those who lived lives in greasy back alleys and smoke-filled doorways earned her the nickname 'the Italian Piaf'. Both Anna and Édith embodied something of their country's spirit and character in their performances, corporeally, and through their lives – expressive, emotional and unafraid.

MERYL STREEP

was directly inspired by Anna's performances

Anna
MAGNANI

ÉDITH PIAF

JOSEPHINE BAKER

COLETTE

are buried in Père Lachaise cemetery, as is Édith

Performed at La Coupole, as did

ISADORA DUNCAN

ÉDITH PIAF is best known for her torch songs. The image of her crooning 'La vie en rose' or 'Non, je ne regrette rien' is deeply embedded in French culture – her colourful life, incredible experiences and emotions infusing every note.

Although all the tales of Édith's childhood should be taken with a hefty pinch of sel, they make for a wonderful story. Named after executed British nurse Edith Cavell, Édith Gassion (the 'Piaf' or 'Sparrow' nickname came later) was born quite literally on the street (or so she liked to claim). She grew up surrounded by extraordinary characters – her grandmother was a brothel keeper, her father and grandfather street acrobats, and her mother a café singer.

As a teenager, she performed alongside her tumbler father, singing in a voice, according to him, loud enough to 'drown out the lions'. By the age of seventeen, she had had a child, who died at the age of two.

She was spotted by nightclub owner Louis Leplée, who dressed her in black and chose for her a repertoire of songs about heartbreak, pain and passion. She went headlong into a recording career. However, Leplée was murdered, and Édith questioned about the crime. To clean up her reputation, she changed her name to Piaf, appeared in Jean Cocteau's play *Le bel indifférent*, and ramped up her singing career.

Soon she became France's most popular entertainer. Tours of Europe followed, and she headlined Carnegie Hall in the USA twice. But two car crashes and years of drinking and prescription drugs took their toll. She died in 1963, and was interred in Paris' famous Père Lachaise cemetery. Although she was denied a Catholic burial at the time, in 2013 the Roman Catholic church gave her a memorial mass. The woman who once said, 'all I've done all my life is disobey' had finally been accepted by the establishment.

Édith was an influence on many musicians and performers, from Elton John to Marianne Faithfull and Lady Gaga. One of her greatest fans is Patti Smith. An unabashed Francophile, who was keen to be a muse, Patti took inspiration from the biography of Piaf, saying, '[She] really dug [her] men and worked for them.' When she moved in with the man who embraced her in this role, Robert Mapplethorpe, one of the first things she did was tack a picture of Édith over her 'makeshift desk'. Later in her career, she'd sing the Sparrow's songs on stage.

Heavily influenced by

NINA SIMONE

A big fan of

FRIDA KAHLO

Bryn Mawr awarded her the Katharine Hepburn Medal

KATHARINE HEPBURN

PATTI SMITH is the point at which the nebulous clouds of rebellion, poetry, art and rock and roll focus into a needle-sharp point.

She was born to a deeply religious family in Chicago, Illinois, but by her teenage years she'd rejected the church and started listening to Bob Dylan records. After college, she moved to Manhattan in New York, where she met photographer Robert Mapplethorpe, with whom she fell in love. Patti became his partner and muse, and they started to create art. He was a fiercely talented photographer, while Patti wrote and performed poems, painted, worked as a journalist, and appeared in plays such as *Cowboy Mouth*, which she co-wrote with Sam Shepard. Mapplethorpe came to realise he was gay, but the pair remained artistic partners and best friends.

In 1974, Patti released a single with a band under the name the Patti Smith Group, who were signed and released their first album, *Horses*, the following year.

The band surfed the New York punk wave, where contemporaries such as The Ramones and Blondie came blinking out of greasy underground clubs like CBGB and Max's Kansas City into the glare of the international spotlight.

In the late 1970s, Patti met Fred 'Sonic' Smith of the proto-punk band MC5, and the pair married and had two children. Patti turned down the volume on her musical career for over a decade, releasing only one album in 1988. The early 1990s was a difficult time for Patti, with the death of Fred, closely followed by that of her brother Todd, but she regrouped and restarted her musical career.

Patti's art was always political, but in her new incarnation she was more radical than ever. She exhibited photographs, published books, curated festivals and received countless honours. A punk polymath, Patti continues to inspire to this day.

At the start of her career, Patti believed she would be an actor, and appeared in several cutting-edge plays. She once claimed that she 'always dreamed of being in *Mother Courage*'. However, her attitude changed when she went twice to see fellow New Jersey girl Meryl Streep perform that role in Central Park. Patti says, 'I couldn't believe how awesome she was. The strength she had but also her movement, her body language.' In turn, Meryl paid tribute to Patti, saying that she saw her as a soulmate and that '[she] would have been quite happy to be Patti Smith'.

SHE MAY hate the description, but Meryl Streep, who has an armful of Oscars and Golden Globes – she's the most nominated actor ever – really is the 'best actress of her generation'.

Meryl began treading the boards in high school plays, and went on to study drama at Yale. She made a name for herself on the stages of New York, in Shakespeare and musicals, but it was watching Robert De Niro's dark, intense performance in Taxi Driver that drew her to film work.

A fierce intelligence and self-belief are the foundations of Meryl's success. According to Meryl, the audition for her breakthrough role in 1979's Kramer vs. Kramer consisted of her telling Dustin Hoffman and the producers of the script's shortcomings – they let her rewrite and improvise her part.

The 1980s saw Meryl rise stratospherically, with lead roles in *The French Lieutenant's Woman*, *Silkwood* and *Out of Africa*. Despite a swerve into lighter parts in the 1990s, her career never faltered.

Meryl's roles contrast wildly: she's appeared in *Adaptation*, *The Devil Wears Prada*, *The Iron Lady* and the huge commercial success of *Mamma Mia!*. She's been garlanded with awards but has never lost her bite. She has described herself as part of 'the left' and, on accepting a lifetime achievement award during the Golden Globes, let rip with an anti-Donald Trump speech, where she said, to rapturous applause, 'When the powerful use their position to bully, we all lose.'

Some of Meryl's finest and most powerful roles have portrayed real-life

Meryl

women: Margaret Thatcher, Julia Child, Karen Silkwood and, in *Suffragette*, Emmeline Pankhurst. She only appears briefly, but her impact can be felt across the film. Meryl explained that the filming of her pivotal scene – a speech Emmeline made on a balcony – affected her deeply: 'To stand on the balcony and look at these uplifted, hopeful young faces, it made me cry. I couldn't get over it. You take your hope from the next generation.' Emmeline's great-granddaughter applauded Meryl's casting, saying, 'How wonderful it is to see Meryl Streep, a staunch feminist herself (whom I'm sure Emmeline would have loved) and a woman not afraid to speak out against Hollywood sexism, play the role of my great-grandmother – a historical feminist icon if ever there was one.'

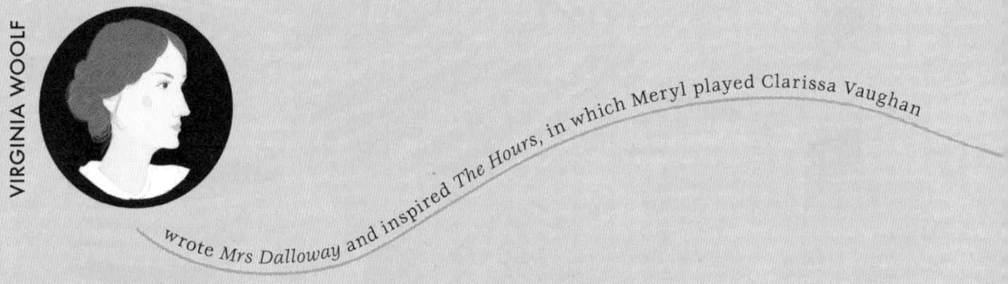

VIRGINIA WOOLF

wrote *Mrs Dalloway* and inspired *The Hours*, in which Meryl played Clarissa Vaughan

Streep

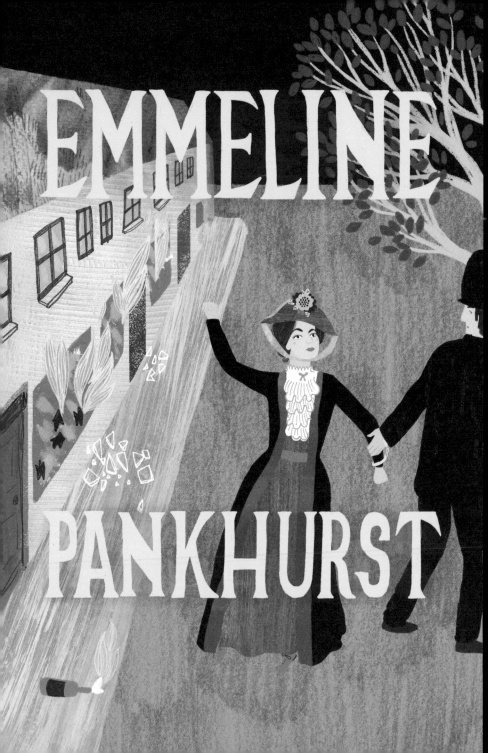

EMMELINE

PANKHURST

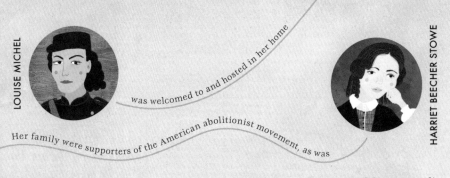

was welcomed to and hosted in her home

Her family were supporters of the American abolitionist movement, as was

UNASHAMEDLY MILITANT, brave and principled, Emmeline (Emily) Pankhurst fought hard for the right of British women to vote, breaking rules and shattering stereotypes as she went.

Born into a Manchester family soaked in radical politics (she went to her first suffrage meeting at fourteen), Emmeline Goulden married Richard Pankhurst, who was twenty-four years her senior and a leading light in the women's suffrage movement. They had five children, but Richard still encouraged Emily to be active in her social work outside the house, and in 1889 they founded the Women's Franchise League, aiming to gain women the right to vote.

Richard died in 1898, and in 1903 Emily set up the all-women, action-focused Women's Social and Political Union (WSPU). Initially organising rallies, petitioning and publishing newsletters, the organisation later used radical methods of protest – arson, widow smashing, rioting and assaulting policemen – to get its point across. Emily believed that the importance of their aims justified their methods, saying, 'Deeds, not words.'

The work of the WSPU escalated after a 500,000-strong march in Hyde Park seemed to have no impact on the government. Women who were repeatedly imprisoned, including Emily, took part in harrowing hunger strikes and were violently force-fed. Some of the group split to form more moderate organisations, but Emily continued on her hard-line path.

During the First World War, Emily put the WSPU's work on hold and concentrated on supporting the war effort. Following the armistice, the 1918 Representation of the People Act granted the vote to women over thirty. After the war, Emily mellowed, and even, to the surprise of many, joined the Conservative party. Weakened by a lifetime of campaigning, imprisonment and hunger strikes, she died in 1928, the same year that all women over twenty-one were awarded the right to vote.

Emily Pankhurst had a close but complex relationship with all her children, but particularly her girls. Christabel, Adela and Sylvia were all involved in the movement, but there was friction between them and Emily about the level of violence they believed suffragettes should use. Adela and Sylvia left the WSPU in 1913. Adela (at the insistence of her mother) emigrated to Australia, while Sylvia became a socialist. Neither daughter shared their mother's enthusiasm for the war – they were pacifists – and when, after a long estrangement, Sylvia met her mother again in 1925, the meeting was strained. Sylvia having a child out of wedlock in late 1927 was believed to have contributed to the stress that caused Emily's death.

SYLVIA PANKHURST never felt the need to fit in. She was deeply artistic, studying at the Manchester School of Art and the Royal College of Art in London. This training made her the perfect person to design logos, flags and banners for her mother's Women's Social and Political Union (WSPU) for which she started to work full-time in 1906. Sylvia was imprisoned and force-fed more than any other suffragette. The 'Cat and Mouse' Act led to her being continually released, then rearrested.

Sylvia was more party political than her mother. A socialist, she was close friends with the Labour party's Keir Hardie, and when she was expelled from the WSPU in 1913, she set up the East London Federation of Suffragettes, which eventually became the Workers' Socialist Federation.

Sylvia believed in universal suffrage, and once she saw the UK suffragettes campaign was likely to succeed, she turned her attention to First World War peace efforts, to her newspaper the *Workers' Dreadnought*, and to mothers' and babies' rights to care.

Towards the end of the conflict she met and began living with Silvio Corio, an Italian anarchist, and their son Richard was born in 1927.

Sylvia's passion for political action never diminished; she campaigned for

worldwide human rights and against oppression. She became a champion of Haile Selassie, the Emperor of Ethiopia, eventually moving there at his request in 1956. Even in later life she was seen as dangerous. MI5 monitored her correspondence and once considered plans for 'muzzling the tiresome Miss Sylvia Pankhurst'. She died in Addis Ababa and received a full state funeral, at which Selassie named her an 'honorary Ethiopian'.

Spending her youth in a house full of political activists shaped and formed the young Sylvia. It wasn't just her immediate family – her mother was keen on inviting other inspiring minds into the house.

One of those people was Louise Michel, a French anarchist who was active in the Paris Commune. Sylvia described her as 'a tiny old woman in a brown cloak, intensely lean, with gleaming eyes and swarthy skin', but still a 'tremendous heroine'.

GEORGE ELIOT

lived on the same road in London, Cheyne Walk

SYLVIA PANKHURST

DEEDS NOT WORDS

VOTES FOR WOMEN

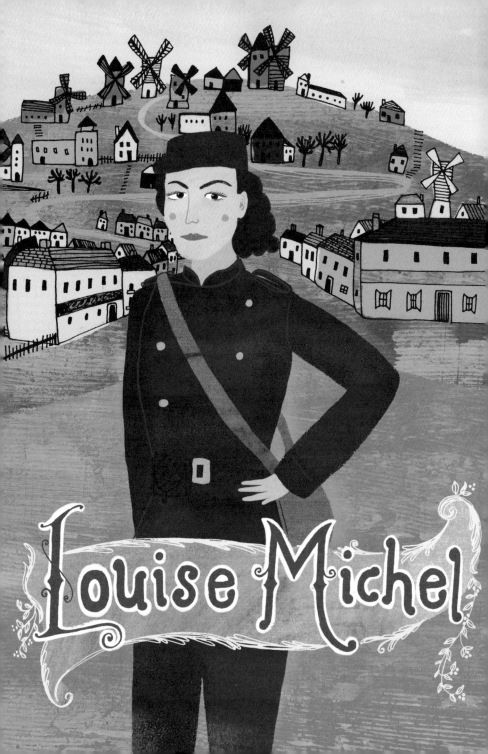

SHE MIGHT peer out of ancient, dog-eared photographs like any other buttoned-up Victorian, but Louise Michel was a gun-toting anarchist known as 'the Red She-wolf' and 'the Red Virgin'. Her early years read like a fairy tale. Born illegitimately to a maid and the local castle-owner's son, she was raised 'idyllically' by her wealthy grandparents, but on their death was driven from the castle by her evil stepmother.

Fending for herself, Louise travelled to Paris, where she wrote poetry and became a teacher in Montmartre. She started attending political meetings and became violently anti-establishment.

In 1871, the National Guard took advantage of the turbulent political consequences of the Franco-Prussian War and established the Paris Commune, a revolutionary government that ruled the city for two-and-a-half months. Louise worked as an ambulance woman for the Commune, where she drafted ostracised prostitutes into service. She also stood on the barricades, gun in hand, wearing a man's uniform and hobnail boots, hair blowing in the wind.

With a reckless contempt for danger, Louise held candles next to piles of flammable weapons to threaten deserters, drank coffee while reading Baudelaire aloud under fire, and played a church organ, drawing the attention of the enemy

– much to the annoyance of her fellow fighters. She saw romance in even the most bloody of situations, later describing the last stand of the Communards at Montmartre cemetery in the most florid terms: 'The clean night air is sweet with the perfume of flowers, and the very tombstones seem alive.'

After the fall of the Commune, Louise was brought to trial, goading the court to sentence her to death. Instead she received twenty months in prison and was deported to New Caledonia, an island east of Australia. Life there wasn't dull – she took the locals' side in a revolt against the French colonials. In 1880, after the Communards were given an amnesty, Louise returned to Paris, where she made speeches and visited London. Age did not mellow her – in 1883 she was imprisoned for leading a mob that pillaged a baker's shop. She howled and roared to the last, and died during a lecture tour in Marseille.

Fighting alongside Louise Michel was Anna Jaclard – a Russian socialist and feminist who was an active member of the Paris Commune, and who was praised by Louise for her bravery during the last days of the insurrection. Anna and Louise were both sentenced to hard labour in the same New Caledonia penal colony, although Anna managed to escape to London and avoid incarceration.

Took part in active warfare, as did

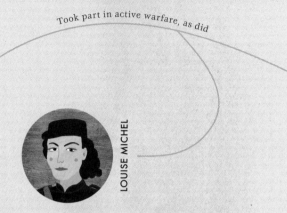

LOUISE MICHEL

A FREE-THINKING radical who didn't shy away from action, Anna was born in Russia into a family of minor royals. Her father was a retired general and, alongside her sister Sofia, she was raised on a diet of political literature. Conversations with two local nihilists transformed her from a spoiled child to an idealistic young woman, dedicated to social and political reform. She secretly published two stories in Dostoevsky's literary magazine Epoch, and went to meet him in Saint Petersburg. He was enraptured and proposed to Anna, but she turned him down, saying, 'His wife must devote herself to him completely and utterly ... And I cannot do that; I want

to live myself!' Despite the rejection, they managed to stay firm friends for life.

Leaving Russia in 1866 for Switzerland, Anna studied medicine in Geneva. Among the exiled radicals she met there was Victor Jaclard, a French anarchist, and the pair joined Marx's First International group. In 1867, they married.

Anna and Victor moved to Paris and became active members of the Paris Commune. Anna fought alongside Louise Michel, Paule Mink and André Léo to establish women's rights, as well as setting up secular schools, ambulance services and work cooperatives. She was described by the secretary of the Russian Embassy

MANUELA SÁENZ

ANITA GARIBALDI

in Paris as a 'harpy' and 'pétroleuse' (a woman who uses petrol to set light to a building).

The Jaclards managed to escape their sentence after the fall of the Commune, travelling from Switzerland to London, where they were sheltered by Karl Marx. In 1874, Anna, accompanied by Victor, returned to Russia, where she settled into a quieter life as a journalist and helped Dostoevsky with translations. It's thought he based the character of Aglaya Epanchin in *The Idiot* on Anna.

Anna's life was entwined with that of her sister, Sofia. Sofia was equally bright, but her interest was piqued by maths. The sisters shared strong beliefs, and their early lives were spent together – Sofia even overheard Anna's rebuttal to Dostoevsky's proposal. Although they eventually led separate lives in Europe, Sofia travelled to Paris to help her sister during the last stand of the Paris Commune, where she saved Victor.

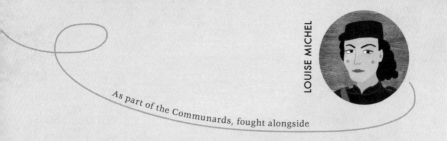

As part of the Communards, fought alongside

SOFIA FOUGHT hard for her education and used her magnificent brain to incredible effect, showing promise from an early age. She claims her father's old calculus notes, which papered her nursery wall, sparked her interest in figures, and by the time she was fourteen she had already taught herself trigonometry.

Sofia desperately wanted to go to university, but the closest that accepted women were in Europe and young women weren't allowed to travel alone. So she arranged a marriage of convenience with her palaeontologist friend Vladimir Kovalevsky, and the pair emigrated to Heidelberg in Germany.

After a stellar stint studying there, the friends moved to Berlin, where Sofia presented three papers that included groundbreaking work on partial differential equations. Despite her incredible achievements, Sofia was unable to find work, so she and Vladimir returned to Russia. There, unexpectedly, they fell in love and had a child. Sofia slowed down a little, but started to write: reviews, fiction, plays and science articles. In time, she returned to her work in maths and, unable to find employment any closer, moved back to Berlin.

Alone in Germany she heard the news that Vladmir had committed suicide after the collapse of his business ventures. Sofia threw herself even harder into her work,

with bittersweet but magnificent results: a tenure at Stockholm University, an editorship of a journal, a chairmanship, the publication of a paper and a play. After another devastating death – this time her sister's – Sofia completed her 'greatest personal triumph', a paper, 'On The Rotation of a Solid Body about a Fixed Point', which won a prestigious prize. Sofia was now at the peak of her academic powers. She met another man, Maksim Kovalevsky, and had a passionate affair, but both were too absorbed in their work to even live in the same country. In 1891, Sofia died, and the world lost an incredible mathematician.

When Sofia was nineteen and living in Heidelberg, she had visited London with Vladimir. He met with Charles Darwin and Thomas Huxley, while she attended the sparkling salons held by George Eliot. Sofia was enchanted by George, saying, 'Never in my life had I heard a softer, more insinuating, more enchanting voice ... I loved her greatly ... the real George Eliot was ten times better than the one I had imagined.' Sofia obviously made a great impression on George, as the book she was writing at the time – *Middlemarch* – contains the somewhat incongruous line, 'In short, a woman was a problem which, since Mr Brooke's mind felt blank before it, could hardly be less complicated than the revolutions of an irregular solid.' Sofia's specialist subject.

WRITER OF some of the finest novels in the English language, George Eliot lived an unconventional and taboo-busting life. Whilst consistently being described as ugly, even by writers who praised her, she was widely regarded as wise and generous. It may have been this very lack of beauty that set her on her stellar journey.

Growing up as Mary Ann Evans in rural Warwickshire, Mary's plainness meant that her father believed she would never marry into money, and so he felt obliged to give her a better education than the vast majority of women.

Her mother died when Mary was in her mid-teens, so she left school to help run her father's household, where she lived until she was thirty. During this time, she became close friends with radical thinkers, who encouraged her to question her well-established religious beliefs. After her father's death, she moved to London.

Mary was made assistant editor of a left-wing newspaper and met philosopher George Henry Lewes, with whom she fell deeply in love. One problem – he was married with children. It was an open marriage, but he could not divorce his wife due to legal issues. Mary and George, nevertheless, considered themselves hitched.

Mary's first work of fiction was the startlingly realistic *Scenes of Clerical Life*, published under the *nom de plume* George Eliot. Her unconventional living arrangements meant that it took a while

for her to be celebrated formally by polite society, but she was eventually accepted. More novels followed, including *Middlemarch* and *The Mill on the Floss*. By this time, George had grown old and frail. Shortly after his death, Mary married John Cross, a man twenty years her junior. She died at the age of sixty-one, and is buried in Highgate cemetery, beside George.

Mary was part of London's progressive Victorian society – the set that held salons, discussed radical thinking and published papers and novels. Another determined thinker and early feminist who mixed in the same circles was physician Elizabeth Garrett Anderson. When Elizabeth set up her hospital, Mary sent two guineas in support of her work.

Defended in an essay by

VIRGINIA WOOLF

QUEEN VICTORIA

asked for her autograph

GEORGE ELIOT

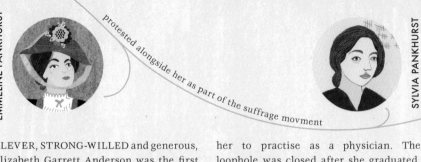

protested alongside her as part of the suffrage movment

CLEVER, STRONG-WILLED and generous, Elizabeth Garrett Anderson was the first female doctor to qualify in England. Bashing down establishment doors and holding them open for other women, she was determined that medical education should be accessible to all.

Born in London, but brought up in Suffolk, Elizabeth received a good education, although she decried the lack of science and maths lessons. She was an admirer of Elizabeth Blackwell, who had qualified to be a doctor in the USA, so travelled to London to meet her. After the meeting, she was determined to become a doctor. Elizabeth and her younger sister Millicent were friends with suffragist and feminist Emily Davies. During a fireside meeting in 1860, the three declared they would promote the cause of women's rights: Elizabeth through the medical profession, Emily through supporting university education for all, and Millicent through politics. They succeeded. Emily went on to found Girton College at Cambridge University, while Millicent – under her married name of Fawcett – became a prominent union leader and suffragette.

As for Elizabeth, with the support of her father she moved to London. Despite her best efforts, no medical school would take her, so she enrolled as a nurse and student. The male students objected to her presence however, and she was forced to leave.

Mischievously, Elizabeth uncovered a loophole at the Society of Apothecaries, and in 1865 passed exams that allowed her to practise as a physician. The loophole was closed after she graduated. The establishment revised its rules to keep women out.

In 1866, Elizabeth opened the St Mary's Dispensary for Women and Children (later renamed The New Hospital for Women), which largely treated victims of the sweeping cholera epidemic. She was able to reward her mentor Blackwell with a post at the hospital – professor of gynaecology. In 1874, she made true on her early promise and founded the London School of Medicine for Women, a place for female physicians to train. She retired with her husband and children to Suffolk in 1902, where she became the first female mayor in England. After her death, the New Hospital was renamed after her.

At the time Elizabeth was applying unsuccessfully for medical courses, she and her friend Emily Davies petitioned the University of London for its degrees to be opened up to women. The pair sent out a circular to influential people asking for their help, among them groundbreaking mathematician Mary Somerville. Mary replied to the circular, lending Elizabeth her support.

Later Elizabeth and Mary's signatures were to appear together on John Stuart Mill's unsuccessful petition for suffrage. The two were not only pioneers in science and maths, but also united by the determination to make the path they'd travelled a little easier for the women who would follow them.

Her book, *Mechanism of the Heavens*, was the direct inspiration for

KNOWN AS 'the queen of nineteenth-century science', Mary Somerville had the alchemic ability to galvanise ideas and theories from different disciplines: maths, astronomy, geography and physics. Her remarkable leaps in thought helped advance science – the word 'scientist' was even coined to describe her, both because 'man of science' seemed wrong and because she worked across disciplines.

Born in Scotland, Mary had the usual education afforded to Victorian girls – she learned needlework, simple maths and a smattering of French. Her interest in maths was sparked by an article in a women's magazine, and by her art tutor's casual mention of geometry while teaching her perspective.

Mary studied obsessively in secret, mastering complex theorems and advanced astronomy, as well as physics. Her marriage to a distant cousin meant it became more difficult to find the opportunity to study, but on his death she had both more time and money to finally indulge herself. Mary's second husband, Dr William Somerville, was much more encouraging. Despite having four children, the two started to ascend into the starriest scientific circles.

In 1835, Mary was elected, alongside her friend Caroline Herschel, as the first female honorary member of the Royal Astronomical Society, and recognised by her peers as a formidable scientific talent. She published papers, written in concise, clear, enthused language, which broke ground in maths and physics, as well as accurately predicting the discovery and placement of Neptune.

Somerville's greatest gift seems to have been this enthusiasm – as well as her outstanding brain she possessed the ability to communicate to others how incredible scientific knowledge is. This talent for exciting others made her an inspiring teacher – so inspiring that one of her pupils, Ada Lovelace, went on to become a world-class mathematician. The two enjoyed a sparkling professional and personal friendship. Ada once wrote in her diary, 'I am going this evening to my friend Mrs Somerville's to stay the night. She has kindly offered to take me to a concert, which my love of music could not resist.' The pair would have made quite a spectacle together: beautiful, fiery Ada and magnetic Mary, rapaciously talking about maths, and laughing into the night.

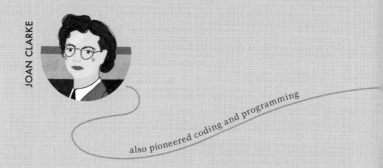

JOAN CLARKE

also pioneered coding and programming

CREATED IN the white-hot crucible of the brief marriage between poet Lord Byron and maths fan Annabella Milbanke, Ada Lovelace's character was a combustible blend of both parents. Her mother was obsessive about Ada's education and, partly because she was worried about her daughter inheriting her father's mental health issues, insisted on giving her a grounding in maths and science – to the exclusion of other subjects. Luckily, Ada loved learning. Even in her spare time she would spend hours doodling and reading about the technological innovations of the Industrial Revolution.

While still a teenager, Ada met fellow mathematician Charles Babbage, who later became known as 'the father of computers' for his work on his Difference and Analytical Engines – machines that could perform mathematical functions. Ada and Charles had similar temperaments and became fast friends. He was fascinated by this young girl who immediately understood his work, calling her 'the Enchantress of Numbers'. They also gained a reputation as two of the worst-dressed people of the nineteenth century.

At the age of nineteen, Ada would meet her future husband, William King, (who became Earl of Lovelace in 1838) and – more significantly – her tutor Mary Somerville.

Ten years after her first encounter with Babbage, Ada translated an Italian article about his engines. She annotated the article with notes, adding in her thoughts and theories about the invention. These notes contain what many consider to be the first computer program. Her great contribution was to think more laterally about how the machines could be used – not just to crunch numbers, but to manipulate symbols and music, and perform a function outside the narrow world of high maths. This lateral thinking is what makes Ada unique – she drew, perhaps, on her more poetic side to envision how the machine might be used creatively and collaboratively.

Tragically, Ada's health began to fail. Despite some interest in electrical experiments and devising a 'calculus of the nervous system', her thoughts became blurred as she self-medicated with opium and wine. She had few friends who understood her mathematical work or who could stop her as she descended into gambling and addiction.

On her death, Ada's friend Florence Nightingale said, 'They said she could not possibly have lived so long, were it not for the tremendous vitality of the brain, that would not die.'

SO MUCH more than 'the lady with the lamp', Florence was the founder of modern nursing; a skilled statistician who invented the polar area diagram and used numbers to shape government policy; and a social reformer who improved healthcare across British society and advocated for positive social change for all women.

Born in Italy but brought up in Derbyshire, Florence was educated by her wealthy father. When she was eighteen, her family toured Europe, where, in Paris, she was introduced to feminism.

Florence believed that she had a calling from God to do something with her life, and it became clear that was nursing. Rejecting marriage, she eventually persuaded her parents to let her train in Düsseldorf, Germany, and at thirty-three

she became superintendent of a hospital for 'gentlewomen' in London.

In 1854, Florence's friend Sidney Herbert sent her and a staff of thirty-eight volunteer nurses to tend to the wounded of the Crimean War. In Scutari, a district of Istanbul in Turkey, they found appalling conditions – not enough medicines, bad hygiene and poor catering facilities. Mass infections were commonplace. Florence learned vital lessons here: that good sanitation, ventilation and nutrition helped save lives. This sparked her focus on sanitary living, which, on her return from war, she introduced into hospitals and working-class homes.

Florence's new celebrity gave her the leverage to make widespread reforms. She wrote a manual on nursing, set up

Florence was the advisor for

a training school and introduced trained nurses into the workhouse system. She inspired nurses in the American Civil War, and advised the US government on field medicine.

Florence and physician Elizabeth Blackwell had a lot in common: they both came from nonconformist, anti-slavery families, and had determined that medicine was the best route out of the prescribed lifestyle for women. When they met in 1850, they bonded immediately,

Florence in awe of the woman who already carried the initials MD.

In 1859 they met again. Florence wanted Elizabeth to be head of her new nursing school, but she refused, convinced that women should be aiming to be doctors. Despite their differences, Florence intervened on Elizabeth's behalf with the president of the General Medical Council, recommending that Elizabeth's name be included on the new British Medical Register.

ELIZABETH GARRETT ANDERSON

hygiene and sanitation at Elizabeth's New Hospital for Women

FLORENCE NIGHTINGALE

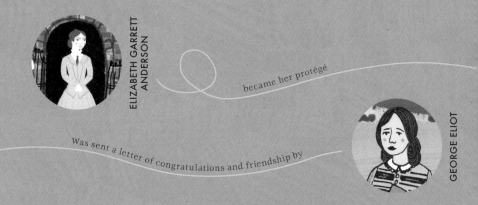

ELIZABETH GARRETT ANDERSON

became her protégé

Was sent a letter of congratulations and friendship by

GEORGE ELIOT

BORN IN Bristol, Elizabeth moved to the USA with her family at the age of eleven. After her anti-slavery activist father's death, the seventeen-year-old Elizabeth started teaching to contribute to the family income. She was inspired to learn about medicine when a close friend who was dying admitted that she might have survived if she'd had access to a 'lady doctor'.

Rejected by Philadelphia's major medical colleges, Elizabeth was finally accepted, due to the unanimous vote of students, by Geneva Medical College in upstate New York. Her fellow, male, students accepted her, but she was regarded as a bizarre sight in the town.

In 1849, Elizabeth became the first woman to gain a medical degree in the United States. She decided to continue her studying in Europe, travelling to Paris, where she enrolled at La Maternité as a student midwife. That same year, she contracted *ophthalmia neonatorum* from a baby and lost sight in one eye, which meant she'd never be able to perform surgery.

Returning to New York, Elizabeth established what became the New York Infirmary for Indigent Women and Children. During the Civil War, the infirmary trained nurses for the Union

effort. At this time she also adopted an Irish orphan, Kitty Barry, who served as a home help and companion until Elizabeth's death.

Elizabeth sought to replicate her successful school model in London. Alongside Elizabeth Garrett Anderson and Sophia Jex-Blake, among others, she established the London School of Medicine for Women in 1874.

Elizabeth retired from medicine three years later and became more active in social reform. She had a very strong Christian moral streak, which she brought to bear on every campaign. Some might have seen her as stubborn and difficult to work with, but it was this focus that had led to Elizabeth having such an astonishing medical career in the first place.

Elizabeth's abolitionist background coloured her life – both she and her siblings carried her father's anti-slavery baton. Her brother, Henry, married Lucy Stone – a prominent suffragist and abolitionist who was closely affiliated with the women's rights movement in the USA from its earliest days. Elizabeth's sister-in-law is credited with directly inspiring one of the women's rights movements leading lights, Susan B. Anthony.

CREDITED WITH gaining American women the right to vote, Susan B. Anthony was a tireless, pragmatic campaigner who used a strong moral compass to guide her drive for social reform.

Susan grew up in a Quaker family steeped in activism: her father had a background in the anti-slavery movement, and she and her siblings inherited his passion for civil rights. Susan helped support her family through teaching and was, at first, tickled by her father's enthusiasm for the nascent women's rights movement. As she explained later: 'I wasn't ready to vote, didn't want to vote, but I did want equal pay for equal work.' However, within a couple of years she was working full-time as a social reformer and public speaker.

Susan was a tireless, resilient campaigner, first for temperance, then women's rights and abolition. She was out on the road in the harshest of conditions to gather signatures for petitions, faced down angry mobs at anti-slavery meetings, endured being pelted with eggs and threatened with guns and knives, and braved the sight of her effigy being dragged through the streets.

The suffrage movement began to splinter into factions, but by the end of the Civil War Susan had emerged as a senior political figure and in-demand speaker. Slowly, state by state, thanks to her tenacity, women won the right to vote. In 1872, Susan was among nearly fifty women in her hometown of Rochester, New York, who attempted to vote. Fifteen

SUSAN B. ANTHONY

managed to mark their papers. Susan was arrested and put on trial, making a now-legendary speech as part of her defence. She was found guilty, but never paid her $100 fine.

Subsequently, Susan's career soared. She spoke globally and set up alliances with women around the world. Her energy never faltered – at the age of seventy-five she explored Yosemite National Park on the back of a mule. She still spoke up to three times a day, and even celebrated her eightieth birthday at the White House. When total women's suffrage was achieved in 1920, it was known as the 'Susan B. Anthony Amendment'.

Susan was a passionate abolitionist and worked for that cause alongside someone born in very different circumstances to her – Harriet Tubman. The two gave speeches at meetings in Rochester together and collaborated on the Underground Railroad, a safe-house route that led slaves to freedom on which Tubman was a 'conductor'. There was an obvious, deep respect between the pair, and Harriet was once referred to by Susan as 'this most wonderful woman'.

Worked alongside and was friends with

Was sent a silver medal by

QUEEN VICTORIA

Quoted as an inspiration to

OPRAH WINFREY

KNOWN AS 'Moses' and 'General Tubman' for her work leading slaves to freedom, Harriet Tubman has become emblematic of the struggle for Black emancipation.

Harriet was born Araminta Ross (Harriet was her mother's name, which she took when she freed herself) into bondage on an estate in Maryland. Suffering years of abuse never deterred her from standing up for those even less fortunate — she once took a severe blow to the head from an angered overseer with a lead weight, intended for another. Amazingly she survived, but she was dogged by pain and narcolepsy for the rest of her life. This injury also gave her hyperreal visions, which she saw as messages from God.

Ill, and worried about being sold on as a sickly inconvenience, Harriet escaped the plantation, using the established network of safe houses and secret routes known as the Underground Railroad. She set up base in Philadelphia, returning to rescue her family, then time and time again to escort more slaves to freedom. They travelled by night, staying in barns, under church floors or in caves, hiding from bounty hunters and marshals. Harriet's secret signal was to sing 'Go Down Moses' at different speeds to indicate if it was safe to proceed.

Despite her lack of formal education, Harriet was a powerful public speaker, and combined practical help with campaigning to formidable effect, drawing on her own experiences. She was brave and committed, and rose from the most humble of beginnings to become an internationally famous activist.

Harriet saw the Civil War as a chance to end the tyranny of slavery, and volunteered as a cook and nurse, then armed scout and spy. She guided a raid that liberated more than 700 slaves. After the war, Harriet married for the second time and adopted a baby girl named Gertie.

Retiring to Auburn, New York, Harriet nursed her parents, whom she had rescued from slavery, and continued to be active in the women's suffrage movement. She died in 1913 after telling family and friends, 'I go to prepare a place for you.'

Standing alongside Harriet in the fight for abolition, and also born into slavery, was Sojourner Truth. The pair had very different approaches to the way they conducted their battles: Harriet was practical, physical and aggressive, helping slaves escape and putting herself in danger, while Sojourner spoke and lectured. Despite fighting for the same cause, the two women met only once, in Boston, Massachusetts in 1864.

harriet
TUBMAN

SOJOURNER

TRUTH

SOJOURNER TRUTH could be described as the mother of intersectional feminism: she showed through her speeches and her deeds that she believed that in order for women to be truly emancipated, everyone, regardless of colour, needed to be heard. She was also notoriously funny, often using satire and sarcasm in her talks to maximise their power.

Isabella Baumfree, as she was first known, grew up in slavery in upstate New York, being bought and sold three times before escaping. She took one daughter with her, but had to leave her other children behind. When she found out that her five-year-old son, Peter, had been illegally sold, she sued her old master and, astonishingly for the time, won.

Isabella became a Christian and moved to New York City, where she spoke at religious revivals, learning quickly how to be an effective and moving orator. She also changed her name to Sojourner Truth. During her preaching travels, she met abolitionists William Lloyd Garrison and Frederick Douglass, who encouraged her to give anti-slavery speeches. She dictated an autobiography, and became interested in the burgeoning women's rights movement.

Sojourner gave her seminal speech, 'Ain't I a Woman', in 1851. In it, she delivered a strong message: that 'woman' often meant 'white woman' and that the emancipation of Black women was as important as the emancipation of everyone.

In 1865, Sojourner anticipated Rosa Parks by ninety years and rode in a whites-only streetcar to force the desegregation of public transport in Washington. She received a dislocated arm for her troubles, but succeeded in her aims. She also tried unsuccessfully to persuade Congress to give ex-slaves land grants to secure private property.

Sojourner continued to speak passionately on subjects including capital punishment until old age made it impossible. During her travels, she met the author of *Uncle Tom's Cabin*, Harriet Beecher Stowe, at Harriet's house, where the writer was hosting a meeting of clergymen and abolitionists. In Harriet's account of the meeting — which has been criticised for stereotyping Sojourner wrongly as a simple southerner, when she was, in fact, a sharp wit from New York State — she portrayed Sojourner as a plain-talking, direct woman with a self-possessed air. She said she had never 'been conversant with anyone who had more of that silent and subtle power which we call personal presence than this woman'.

UNCLE TOM'S CABIN was the book that sent shockwaves through a continent, put a spark to the tinder of the American Civil War and changed thousands of lives. Harriet Beecher Stowe not only wrote it, but put the anger she felt while composing it into direct action.

Harriet's family had strong roots in the Calvinist church and abolitionist movements, and she and her twelve siblings were encouraged to make the most of their education and become involved in public affairs. All seven of her brothers became preachers, whilst the sisters were emboldened to aim high and fight against prejudice. Harriet's sister Catharine founded an academically focused girls' school, which Harriet attended.

When she was twenty-one, Harriet moved with her father to Cincinnati, Ohio, where she was to meet her husband as well as many others who shared her radical views (some of whom were active in the Underground Railroad). There she started writing.

It was the passing of the Fugitive Slave Law, punishing anyone who helped escaped slaves and giving slave owners more rights, that so incensed Harriet. Now in Maine and grieving her seventh and youngest child, she published *Uncle Tom's Cabin* in installments in the anti-slavery newspaper, *National Era*. It was instantly popular, and in 1852 was published in book form. It went on to worldwide success and was, according to some, the bestselling book after the Bible in the nineteenth century.

Its impact was seismic. Harriet had succeeded in humanising the effects of slavery in heartbreaking fashion. Unaware of the horrors unfolding in the South, those in the northern states were jolted from their ignorance; even President Lincoln demanded to meet with Harriet. After the Civil War, Harriet continued to write, edit magazines and campaign.

Latterly the book became controversial – some saw the characters as subservient and childlike, and argued that their depiction reinforced racial stereotypes. However, in recent years, the work has been re-evaluated and recognised as a vital step in the path towards abolition.

On its first day of publication, Harriet sent a copy of her book to Prince Albert, in England. The royal family became fans, and on a visit to England a discreet meeting between Queen Victoria and Harriet was arranged. Stowe's carriage passed Victoria's on the road, and the two women silently nodded to each other in mutual admiration.

EMMELINE PANKHURST and family worked closely with Harriet's family as part of the abolitionist movement

BEECHER STOWE

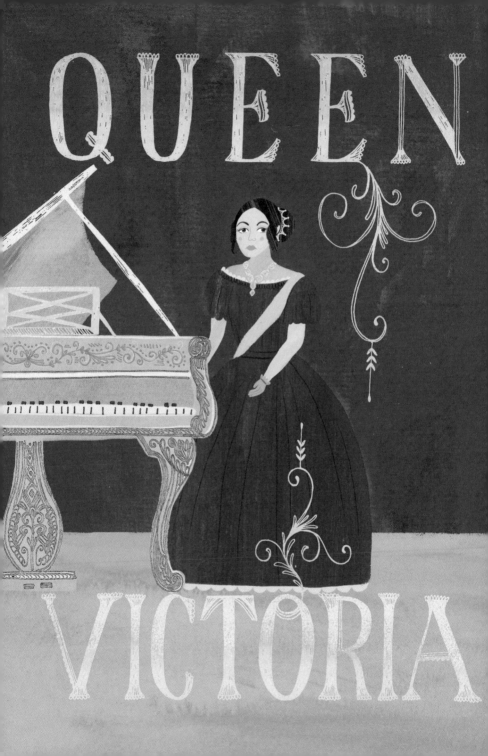

THE EMBODIMENT of strict moral values, decorum and propriety, Alexandrina Victoria was the figurehead of the British Empire and its empire. She restored respectability to a tarnished royal family, established and cemented relations both dynastically and politically across Europe, and ruled over a country that was transforming into a globally important powerhouse of industry.

Life for young Victoria was quiet. Her uncle was king, and it was thought unlikely that she would ever have to reign as a monarch. She spoke German as a first language, though mastered English early, and was described as mischievous and graceful. By her teenage years, after the deaths of her father and two elderly uncles, it was apparent that she'd have to rule, and she became the lynchpin of behind-the-scenes power struggles, plots and politics.

When Victoria was eighteen, her last surviving uncle died and she was made queen. She married her cousin, Prince Albert of Saxe-Coburg and Gotha, shortly after – it was a tempestuous relationship but very loving, and resulted in nine children.

Victoria was good at taking counsel and learned the art of politics fast, steering the country through a number of constitutional crises. She and Albert, very aware of a growing republican movement, made huge efforts to support charities and institutions publicly. She was good at international PR, too, making crowd-pleasing trips to France and Ireland. Victoria oversaw huge advances in technology during her reign. Trains and ships connected cities at home and abroad, and solidified the empire. She strengthened ties with Canada, Australia and India while acquiring swathes of territory in Africa.

When Victoria was forty-two, her beloved Albert died and her world came to a shuddering halt. Victoria was inconsolable. She went into mourning, wearing black for the next thirty-nine years of her life. She continued with her duties, and helped hold the country together through some shaky political administrations, but there was forever a sadness about her.

Victoria loved music, especially opera. She adored singing and was an accomplished piano player – she owned a gilded Bechstein piano. Her favourite composer was Felix Mendelssohn and, as the queen, she could indulge her passion by inviting him to the palace. On a visit in 1842, she insisted on singing one of her favourite of his songs, 'Italien', to him. Embarrassingly, Felix had to admit that he wasn't the writer of the song – it was the work of his sister, Fanny. Felix had 'honoured' Fanny by performing the song – in those days, women weren't considered capable of being composers.

RECOGNISED AS a significant composer only long after her death, it was Fanny Mendelssohn's perseverance and talent, combined with a tenaciously supportive husband, that resulted in her writing complex and adventurous pieces.

Fanny and her brother, the composer Felix, grew up in Hamburg, Germany as fast friends. Both were obsessed with music, learning how to compose together. Fanny was regarded as a prodigy. Her teacher, Carl Friedrich Zelter, described how she could 'play like a man' – the highest accolade at the time. At the age of fourteen, she memorised all Bach's Preludes and Fugues, which she played for her father's birthday.

At the age of seventeen, Fanny met painter Wilhelm Hensel, who quickly fell in love with her. Wilhelm was the butt of the Mendelssohn family's jokes — they laughed at his stupidity and lack of musical ability — but while Felix was away on his European tour, Wilhelm returned and courted Fanny. He was in awe of her talents and they wed on his condition that she carried on composing. Every morning of their marriage, he'd give her a blank manuscript, and he expected it to be filled on his return from his studio.

Fanny gradually began to gain in confidence, and started to host private concerts for her pieces. She made one public appearance in 1838, playing one of her brother's compositions, and, in 1846, published some of her own works, collected as her Op.1. Tragically, just as her professional career was starting to blossom, she died of a heart attack. Her brother died a year later. Latterly, her music has had a reappraisal. Her long-lost Easter Sonata was discovered in a private collection in 1970 and, although initially credited to her brother, is now performed as her work.

Felix's continuous, rather cruel dismissals of Fanny's talents were perhaps due more to her status as his sister, rather than as a woman – he encouraged other female composers and performers. He often played alongside Clara Wieck Schumann, pianist and composer. Clara became a close friend of Fanny, describing her as 'undoubtedly the most distinguished woman musician of her time'.

A BRILLIANT pianist and composer, Clara sidelined her career to nurture her husband Robert Schumann's talents. His mental health issues, and her reported affairs with fellow composers Johannes Brahms and Theodor Kirchner, made for a melodramatic, vivid life, soundtracked by soaring strings and throbbing bass.

Born in Leipzig, Germany, to an opera singer and a distinguished music teacher, Clara lived in the care of her father after her parents' divorce. Friedrich Wieck hothoused Clara using his own musical teaching methods, and by the age of eleven she was touring Europe as a pianist, performing for celebrities including Goethe and Paganini and receiving critical acclaim. By the time she was eighteen, the likes of Chopin and Liszt had also become fans.

Robert Schumann was another member of the Wieck household. He was a live-in student of Wieck's, who'd moved in when Clara was nine. Much to her father's horror, when Clara was eighteen she accepted Robert's proposal of marriage. Friedrich panicked and sent Clara off to live in Dresden, kicked Robert out of the house, and hastily arranged a packed performance schedule for his daughter. But the star-crossed pair continued their contact via letters. After a legal battle over Clara, the couple married a day before her twenty-first birthday. They went on to have eight children.

Unlike her father, who had incredibly high expectations of his daughter, Schumann wasn't hugely supportive of Clara's career. Yes, he helped her find publishers for her work, but Clara was to play second fiddle to the great Schumann. The pair nurtured the careers of violinist Joseph Joachim and pianist Johannes Brahms, whose work Clara premiered and with whom it is thought she had an affair.

NINA SIMONE

A fiercely skilled classical pianist, as was

Brahms once wailed in a letter to his love, 'Can't you remove the spell you have cast over me?' Clara was also said to have had a liaison with one of Brahms' best friends, composer Theodor Kirchner.

Robert's mental health was fragile; he tried to commit suicide by throwing himself into the Rhine, and ended up in a sanatorium. Clara increasingly relied on the support of friends, who included Mendelssohn, Brahms and opera singer Jenny Lind – even more so after her husband's death when she was thirty-seven.

Cheeringly, Clara's work was re-evaluated in her lifetime, during the 1870s. She resumed her performance tours after Robert's death and, in 1878, became a piano teacher at the Hoch Conservatory in Frankfurt. She died in Frankfurt in 1896.

The dark, troubled life of Robert Schumann and the complicated love affairs of his wife make for a fascinating story, and in 1947 the film *Song of Love* attempted to tell the tale. Paul Henreid played Schumann and Katharine Hepburn took the role of Clara. Katharine learned to play piano for the role, but the film was not a huge success due, in part, to Katharine's principled, off-screen, public opposition to the anti-communist movement in Hollywood.

SALTY, BOISTEROUS Katharine Hepburn never let Hollywood tame her headstrong spirit. Wisecracking, generous and loyal to her friends, her talent combined with an intelligence and sense of humour that proved irresistible to audiences for over eight decades. Plus, she looked great in a pair of slacks.

Born to a suffragette and a doctor, Katharine's childhood was full: she went on demonstrations, swam in rivers, played sports. But her life became irreversibly darker after the suicide of her beloved elder brother, whose hanged body Katharine found. Her consequent scorn of fuss and emotions was attributed to the incident.

Graduating with a history and philosophy degree from Bryn Mawr, Katharine headed for the theatre, where she 'glowed' on stage. Her gutsy attitude made her difficult to direct, but brought an assurance to her acting. Her first Hollywood film was *A Bill of Divorcement*, opposite John Barrymore, for which she received stellar reviews. She won an Academy Award for her third film, *Morning Glory*, the first of four. She was persistent. After a string of flops led to her being labelled 'box office poison', she bought up the rights to the play *Holiday*, the film of which went on to be a commercial success.

Katharine's stridently liberal, pro-choice, atheist views influenced the roles she took. Her characters were strong and witty but with a human side: Jo March in *Little Women*, Susan Vance in *Bringing Up Baby*, Tracy Samantha Lord in *The Philadelphia Story*. Her career continued to dazzle, as she starred in some of the greatest movies of all time: *The African Queen*, *Guess Who's Coming to Dinner*, *On Golden Pond*. She weathered the anti-communist storm in Hollywood, and

KATHARINE HEPBURN

went on to promote birth control and pro-choice causes.

Katharine had married a stockbroker at the age of twenty-one, but found the union constricting; the pair divorced amicably six years later. Katharine's sex life has been the source of much speculation. It's thought she was probably bisexual, but she had a string of high-profile male lovers: Howard Hughes, John Ford and, most famously, Spencer Tracy, with whom she had a twenty-six-year affair.

She died in her beloved family home in Connecticut at the age of ninety-six.

In 1943, Katharine appeared in *Stage Door Canteen*, a propaganda film set in a New York nightclub where servicemen are entertained by US celebrities. Its format lent itself to cameo roles; Katharine makes an appearance as herself. Other luminaries drop in: Harpo Marx, Tallulah Bankhead, Gracie Fields and Gypsy Rose Lee, who, controversially, performs a striptease in front of Allied flags. Her routine was called 'Psychology of a Strip-Tease Dancer', and featured *Gypsy* debating philosophy, art and literature, all while seductively removing her clothing.

ELSA SCHIAPARELLI

designed clothes she loved

GALA DALÍ

LEONORA CARRINGTON

JOSEPHINE BAKER

Was painted by Max Ernst, who had affairs with

Became the top-billed artist in the Ziegfeld Follies, as was

BORN ROSE Louise Hovick, Gypsy Rose Lee didn't become famous for taking off her clothes, but for the *way* she took off her clothes. She was likeable – women adored her as much as men – funny and approachable, but with a confident poise. Her shockingly honest memoir, *Gypsy*, was turned into one of the all-time great musicals.

The Hovick family was legendarily dysfunctional and Rose Hovick was the original monstrous stage mother. She faked her children's birth certificates and corralled Gypsy's older sister June into supporting the family by dancing on vaudeville stages at the age of two and a half. Gypsy was considered less talented, and was left behind when her mother and sister went on the road, but still ended up as a chorus girl. She started her burlesque career when a dress strap gave way, and developed a style that was more tease than strip, cracking jokes as she did it and reciting intellectual passages. She soon became a huge star, the main draw of the sophisticated Minsky's Burlesque, coyly dropping pins from her dress into a tuba to make a ting and taking fifteen minutes to remove a single glove.

However, even at the height of Gypsy's career, her nightmare mother continued to demand money. Gypsy rented a large apartment for her in Manhattan, New York, where Rose went on to shoot and kill her female lover. She was also rumoured to have killed a hotel manager by pushing him out of the window. When Rose died of cancer in 1954, her final malicious words to her daughter were, 'You'll never forget how I'm holding you right this minute, wishing with all my heart I could take you all the way down with me.'

Gypsy's intellectual shtick was more than on-stage banter. She ran with the cultural and literary elite — Benjamin Britten, Leonard Bernstein, W.H. Auden and Joan Miró were friends, while Otto Preminger fathered her child. She was political, too, supporting the Popular Front in the Spanish Civil War.

Towards the end of her life, Gypsy presented a TV show, where her quick wit was put to good use. She died at the age of fifty-nine.

Gypsy was well and truly part of the Hollywood set, where she made friends with actress Hedy Lamarr. Hedy once said, a little fruitily, 'One of my favourite people is Gypsy Rose Lee. She bears out the Biblical promise that he who has, gets. And I hope she gets a lot more.'

had a relationship with Howard Hughes, who also dated

FROM BEING the first woman to simulate an orgasm in a non-pornographic film and escaping a marriage to a dastardly Nazi arms dealer, to inventing the technology that became the foundation of Wi-Fi and Bluetooth, Hedy Lamarr shattered twentieth-century stereotypes in the most extraordinary way in a dazzlingly luminescent life story, which even the furthest-fetched film script would find hard to match.

Born Hedwig Eva Kiesler in Vienna, Austria, the young Hedy's porcelain skin, glossy black hair and infinity pool eyes attracted the attentions of many men, including villainous Friedrich Mandl, third-richest man in the country and arms dealer to Benito Mussolini and Adolf Hitler. Kept in a gilded cage at Schloss Schwarzenau after their marriage, the endless socialising with weapons makers did, however, spark Hedy's interest in technology.

Hedy fled to London where she met the head of MGM, Louis B. Mayer. Seeing her potential as the next Greta Garbo, Mayer contracted her. Hedy's dark, European-style beauty was seen as exotic in the cornbread USA. After failed attempts to tame her with wigs and bland outfits, she kept her signature look, which she put to mesmerising use in her role in *Algiers*. It sent her straight into the Hollywood stratosphere.

As time went on, Hedy grew frustrated with her parts' lack of depth, declaring,

'Any girl can be glamorous. All you have to do is stand still and look stupid.'

She filled her time inventing a glow-in-the-dark dog collar, cubes that turned water into cola and a project based on fragments gleaned from conversations at Schwarzenau. With technical input from composer George Antheil, Hedy patented a 'secret communications system' based on frequency hopping and meant for radio-guided missiles. The twosome gave the invention to the US Navy for free, but it mouldered in their files for decades.

However, it later formed the basis for today's communications technology, including phones, Wi-Fi and GPS systems.

Hedy was belatedly recognised for her scientific achievements: in 1997 she won the Electronic Frontier Foundation Pioneer Award and the Bulbie Gnass Spirit of Achievement Bronze Award. She didn't attend the ceremonies, however, as by that time she had become a recluse. Posthumously, she was inducted into the National Inventors Hall of Fame — overdue recognition for a soaring mind hidden from the world behind incandescent beauty.

Like Hedy Lamarr, Joan Clarke would remain unrecognised for her scientific innovation for decades after VE Day. She stood alongside thousands of other women who, despite not being allowed to fight on the front line during the Second World War, made brave and vital contributions to the war effort.

JOAN CLARKE'S modesty and enviable ability to keep a secret means that we'll never really know the extent of her contributions to codebreaking in the Second World War. Winston Churchill once described those who worked on cracking cyphers during the conflict as, 'The geese that laid the golden eggs and never cackled.'

Born to a vicar and his wife in London, Joan Clarke was a formidable mathematician. She graduated with a double first from Cambridge University – although women weren't awarded full degrees until 1948 – and was recruited to the top-secret Government Code and Cypher School at Bletchley Park, just outside London, in 1939. Twelve thousand people worked at Bletchley, 8,000 of them women. Most of them were in repetitive checking and transcribing jobs, but Joan

was fast-tracked from a secretarial role to working in the research team, based in Hut 8. Joan was classified as a linguist, as there were no provisions in place for a senior female cryptanalyst. She took pleasure in filling in forms, 'grade: linguist, languages: none'.

It was here that Joan met Alan Turing, a shy man with an equal gift for maths. The two were very similar – both liked chess, puzzles and nature — and they became close friends. Despite Turing being gay, they even became engaged for a while, until he terminated the arrangement, believing he'd make Joan unhappy. They stayed friends until his death.

The work the pair did was complicated and vitally important. The team broke new codes daily, transcribing messages in real time and saving lives and equipment in the process.

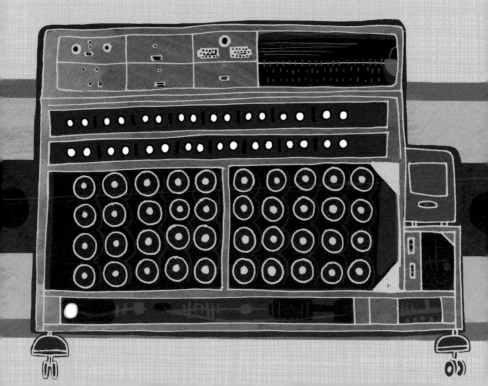

After the war, Joan received an MBE, married a retired army officer she had worked alongside at Bletchley, and moved to Scotland. She had a quiet existence, spending time researching Scottish coinage and knitting – a secretive end to a life spent cracking secrets. She died in 1996.

Joan was one of thousands of women who made a direct contribution to winning the war. Fighting alongside her, for the same cause, albeit in a much more palpable way, was pilot Amy Johnson. Like Joan's, much of Amy's work in the war was hush-hush – even the reason for her final flight is still a government secret.

also pioneered coding and programming

ADA LOVELACE

JOAN

CLARKE

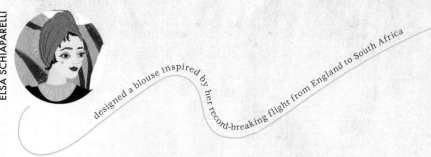

designed a blouse inspired by her record-breaking flight from England to South Africa

AMY WAS working as a legal secretary when her interest in flying was piqued by a chance Sunday afternoon trip to the Stag Lane aerodrome in north London. She later wrote, 'Had I been a man, I might have explored the Poles or climbed Mount Everest, but as it was my spirit found outlet in the air.' Unlike many titled and rich dilettante flyers, Amy had bigger plans than simply soaring around for larks. She hatched a plan for her first daring record-breaking attempt – an epic solo trip from the UK to Australia. Astonishingly, before she set off she'd only amassed a measly eighty-five hours of flying practice.

Our heroine soared away from Croydon aerodrome on 5 May 1930 in a second-hand Gipsy Moth called *Jason*, which her father helped her to buy. Her *Girl's Own* adventure took her in a naively drawn straight line across sandstorm-whipped deserts, through Indian monsoons and over mountains rough with thermals. The world's press was fascinated and, although she didn't break the existing record, by the time she crash-landed in Darwin she was internationally famous. She was awarded a CBE by King George V.

In 1932, Amy gained a new co-pilot and husband, Jim Mollison, who proposed to her only eight hours after they met. The pair went on to fly the Atlantic, where they set a record for flying from Britain to America and were welcomed with a New York ticker-tape parade.

However, racing and daring deeds didn't pay the rent, so Amy started writing and dabbled in the fashion industry – Elsa Schiaparelli even designed a collection inspired by her adventures.

During the Second World War, Amy joined the newly formed Air Transport Auxiliary (ATA), which transported RAF aircraft around the UK. The ATA's female members were christened the 'Attagirls' and became the first women to receive equal pay in a government position. On Sunday 5 January 1941, Amy was on a mission to deliver an Airspeed Oxford from Blackpool to Oxfordshire when she crashed into the sea off Herne Bay and went missing, presumed drowned. Mystery surrounds her death, and her body was never recovered. Amy perhaps provided her most apposite epitaph herself, once remarking, 'I am an ordinary woman who did extraordinary things.'

Amy had a great deal in common with pioneering French pilot Hélène Dutrieu – both were world record breakers, both worked during world wars and both worked as writers. They also each had an eye for haute couture fashion. In 2003, both Amy and Hélène were named by Women in Aviation International as two of the 100 most influential women in the aviation and aerospace industry.

ADDICTED TO speed and adrenaline, Hélène Dutrieu careered in breakneck style from the nineteenth to the twentieth century with a grin, a can-do attitude and, most shockingly, no corset. At a time when many women were constrained by long skirts and overbearing men, she was a cycling champion, a stunt rider, a car racer and a pioneer of aviation.

Born in Belgium, Hélène left school at fourteen. Inspired by a daredevil elder brother, she became a racing cyclist, breaking the women's world record for distance cycled in one hour in 1893. But flat courses weren't enough to satisfy her adventurous urges, so she became a stunt rider, inventing 'La Flèche Humaine' ('The Human Arrow') – a trick where she jumped over 15 metres on her bike.

Hélène was a performer, and following a crash in Berlin she put this sense of showbiz to work while she recovered her health, appearing on stage as a comedy actress. By this time she was a celebrity, loved for her aesthetic, chirpiness and bravery. She was also small-framed and skinny. All these elements made her the perfect choice for Clément-Bayard to launch their new aeroplane, the Santos-Dumont Demoiselle No 19. The thinking behind the choice was patronising at best: if a slender woman can fly our plane, a man will find it easy. However, not many men had the guts and skills to match Hélène.

By 1910, Hélène had become the first woman to fly with a passenger. In November of that year she became the fourth woman in the world to earn a pilot's licence. Her 'Human Arrow' nickname was replaced by another, equally dashing nomenclature: 'Lady Hawk'.

Hélène, who wore elegant flying suits, was renowned for her sense of style, but a clothing-based scandal struck her in 1910, when it emerged that she – quelle horreur – didn't wear a corset while flying. However, Hélène shrugged off the outrage. She retired from her triumphant aeronautical career in 1913, having been awarded the Légion d'Honneur.

During the First World War, Dutrieu put her sharply honed driving abilities to practical use, becoming an ambulance driver and then serving as the director of a military hospital. After the war, she became a journalist, and also set up the Coupe Hélène Dutrieu-Mortier – awarded to the French or Belgian female pilot who made the year's longest non-stop flight. Dutrieu was one of the most influential female pilots of the early twentieth century, blazing the way for others to follow in her flight path.

The Femina Cup was an award established in 1910 given to the female pilot with the longest flight made that year. The first formal winner was Hélène. She won the award the next year too. However, her close challenger for both cups was French pilot Marie Marvingt, who had, in fact, been named prematurely as the winner of the first cup, but was beaten in the dying days of 1910 by Hélène's longer flight.

Pioneered advances in nursing technology, as did

Received the Croix de Guerre for services to the French Air Force in WWII, as did

MORE PLATINUM than iron woman, Marie Marvingt was a world-beater at any sport she turned her hand to. Encouraged by her postmaster father to excel physically, at the age of five the tiny Marie could swim 4,000 metres in a day. At fifteen, she canoed over 400 kilometres from Nancy in France to Koblenz in Germany. By the time she was an adult, she'd scaled many of Switzerland's most challenging peaks, had become the first woman to swim the length of the Seine through Paris, was garlanded for shooting, and had beaten the rest of the world at winter sports and bobsled. In 1908, Marie attempted to enter the Tour de France, but was refused as she was a woman. Undeterred, she cycled the course after the riders. Only thirty-six of the 114 male competitors completed the course; Marie beat several of their times.

Marie was not content to contain her achievements to land, she became the first woman to pilot a balloon across the North Sea and English Channel, then focused her sights on the new way to soar like a bird: the aeroplane.

By November 1910, Marie had earned a pilot's licence and become the first woman to fly solo in a monoplane. She loved flying long distances, competing for the Femina Cup, as well as appearing at air displays. It was at this time that she proposed the development of an air ambulance division to the French government. They weren't interested in her idea, but Marie didn't give up, even designing and ordering a prototype.

Marie was unstoppable. During the First World War, she desperately wanted to enter military service, so she disguised herself as a man and fought on the front lines. She was discovered, but continued working as a Red Cross nurse. By 1915, she was rumoured to have become the first woman to fly in combat, bombing Metz, for which she received the Croix de Guerre.

It was the air ambulances that continued to fascinate and obsess Marie. She dedicated her post-war life to speaking and advocating for their use. She created awards for air ambulance design, established the civil air ambulance in Morocco, and developed training courses for 'nurses of the air'. Only in 1939 did the government grasp how forward-thinking her ideas were, and her input was vital to establishing l'aviation sanitaire, which used female pilots and nurses to treat casualties. Even more radically, the government also set up a corps of female military pilots, who followed the flight path traced by Marie. Among them was experienced flyer Maryse Hilsz, who was appointed a second lieutenant.

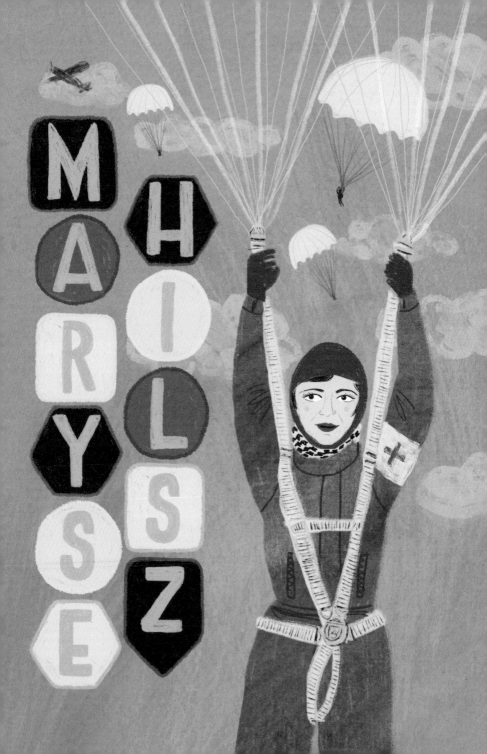

ANNE FRANK

JOSEPHINE BAKER

A member of the European Resistance in WWII alongside

AUDREY HEPBURN

MARYSE HILSZ packed more into her thirties and early forties than most women do in a lifetime, putting her passion for flight above relationships and, ultimately, her life.

Maryse was a milliner, but her passion was always for aviation. In her twenties, she entered a parachute competition, despite having never been on board a plane. She got the jumping bug and started leaping professionally, as well as wing walking, in order to finance getting her pilot's licence.

Within three years of getting her licence, the elegant, strong-willed Maryse was making waves. She flew to Saigon and back, and broke speed and distance records flying to and from Tokyo. In 1936, she reached an altitude of 14,310 metres in a plane with a propeller – an achievement still unbeaten by any woman. She often flew alone, having to mend her aeroplane herself, and once had to use her emergency ejector seat during a speed record attempt.

In her early thirties, Maryse met fellow aviator André Salel. They immediately fell into a passionate love affair, but, in a dramatic pact, they decided to never get married, both terrified that their adventurous lives would be compromised if they settled down. In 1934, André's plane crashed and he and his mechanic were killed. A devastated Maryse erected a stone in his honour.

During the Second World War, Maryse joined the resistance, flying covert missions and once making an emergency landing in Turkey. After the war, she joined the French Air Force, where she headed up an elite group of female flyers. Her hunch that her adventurous lifestyle would mean a short life proved to be true: in 1946, Maryse died in a crash with three other crew members while piloting through bad weather.

In 1933, Maryse was named joint Woman of the Year by the Fédération Aéronautique Internationale. She shared the honour with Amelia Earhart.

PERHAPS THE most well-known female pilot in history, Amelia Earhart was fearless in the air and on the ground, backing women's rights as well as commercial flights. She remains an icon of all-American adventure and spirit.

Rat-shooting, toad-keeping young Amelia revelled in her childhood freedom. Her first 'flight' was from the top of her garden shed on a home-made rollercoaster. She coupled her love of danger with admiration for high-achieving women, keeping a scrapbook of her favourites.

On leaving school in 1916, Amelia worked as a volunteer in a military hospital, but caught pneumonia, during her convalescence, she watched a display by a First World War pilot, piquing her interest in flight. A trip in a small plane clarified everything, and she knew she had to fly.

Amelia worked at different jobs to pay for her lessons. She cut her hair short and roughed up her leather jacket, then bought a plane and got her licence in 1923. She progressed fast – in 1928 she was sponsored by rich heiress and committed feminist Amy Phipps Guest to fly as a passenger across the Atlantic Ocean. This trip made Amelia an instant celebrity, able to take advantage of sponsorship from the likes of Lucky Strike cigarettes.

Amelia became an official of the National Aeronautic Association, where she lobbied for women-only records, and in 1932 she was the first woman to pilot a plane solo across the Atlantic. Her numerous achievements made her a poster girl for other female flyers, and many of the flights she took soon became established commercial air routes.

Amelia's dream was to fly around the world. Her first attempt was aborted when she crashed on take-off. Undeterred, she tried again. On 2 July 1937, on the leg between New Guinea and Howland Island in the Pacific, she and her navigator lost radio contact and, despite desperate searches, they were never heard from again.

Amelia did, however, leave a powerful legacy, inspiring many women to fly. She once said, 'Women must try to do things as men have tried. When they fail, their failure must be but a challenge to others.'

One of Amelia's fastest friends was politician, diplomat and activist Eleanor Roosevelt. The two met in 1932, and would sneak out of the White House together to go to parties and take flying trips in evening dresses, when Amelia would let Eleanor take control of the plane for a few minutes. Eleanor was inspired by Amelia to learn to pilot, but, after getting a permit, she never got off the ground. The two were advocates for women's causes and supported each other's organisations. True kindred spirits.

HUMANITARIAN, ACTIVIST and writer, Eleanor Roosevelt was also the longest-serving first lady of the USA. Her intellect, empathy and energy enabled her to set the standards by which other presidents' wives will forever be judged.

A niece of President Theodore Roosevelt, by the age of ten Eleanor had lost both her mother and brother to diptheria, and her alcoholic father to an accident-induced seizure. She was a serious child, aware of her responsibilities, and found a kindred spirit in the feminist headmistress of her finishing school.

At nineteen, Eleanor met Franklin D. Roosevelt, a distant cousin, with whom she would go on to share a marriage of forty years and six children. Their romantic relationship was strained by Franklin's infidelities, but politically and professionally Eleanor stood beside him. She had a series of intense friendships with women, with at least one – with journalist Lorena Hickok – thought to be a full-blown relationship.

Eleanor was a permanent presence beside Franklin on the campaign trail, often making speeches or appearances on his behalf. She was an excellent campaigner, working for the Democratic party alongside her day job teaching at a girls' school. She had to give up that job when Franklin became president but, unlike previous first ladies, Eleanor continued the work she had started before the move to the White House. She spoke at conventions, wrote a magazine column and had her own radio show.

Eleanor soon began to immerse herself in activism, fighting for the rights of youth groups, establishing communities for miners blacklisted due to union activity, opposing Japanese-American internment camps, and becoming a figurehead for the burgeoning civil rights movement. She preferred to work towards self-sufficiency rather than heading up patronising charities.

During the Second World War, Eleanor worked tirelessly to boost morale among troops and to encourage women into war work. Following Franklin's death in 1945, just five months before the end of the war, she was appointed as a delegate to the United Nations and, in 1947, made the chairperson of the United Nations Commission on Human Rights; two truly heavyweight roles. She also continued her campaigning in the Democratic party and her social activism. She died at the age of seventy-eight in New York City.

One of Eleanor's closest friends was journalist and editor Marie Mattingly Meloney. On Marie's death, Eleanor wrote: 'She believed that women had an important part to play in the future … She helped many little people like myself to feel that we had a contribution and an obligation to try to grow.'

Worked on a public information film about the excellence of American women with her friend

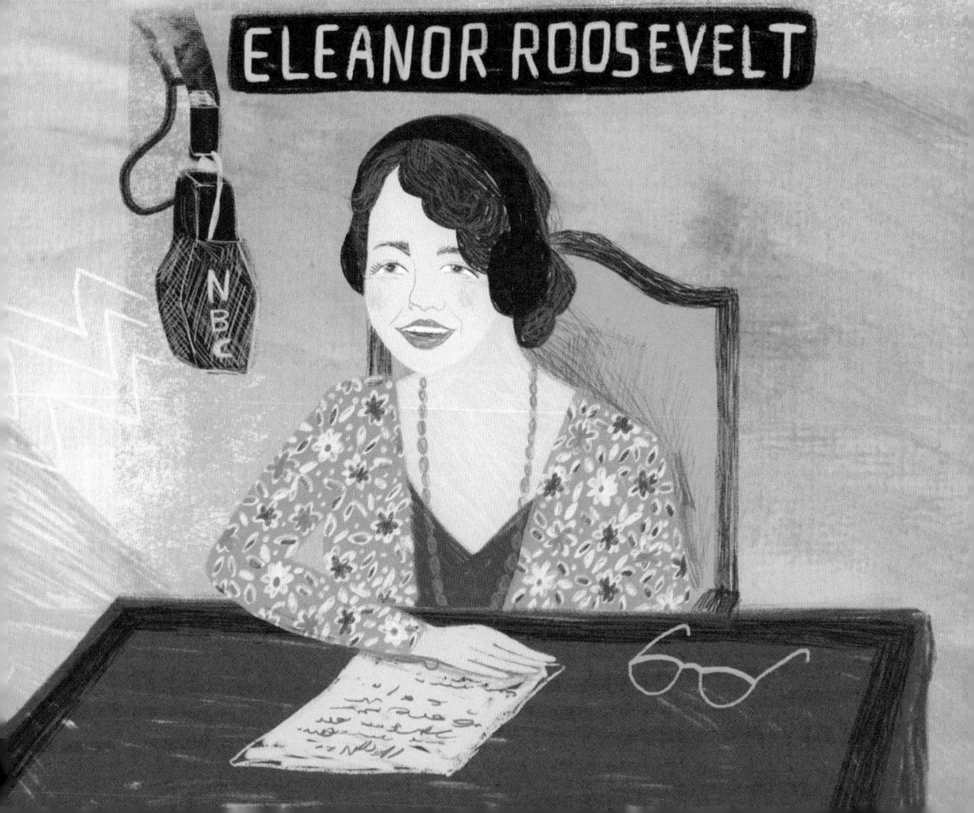

KATHERINE HEPBURN

ELEANOR ROOSEVELT

NBC

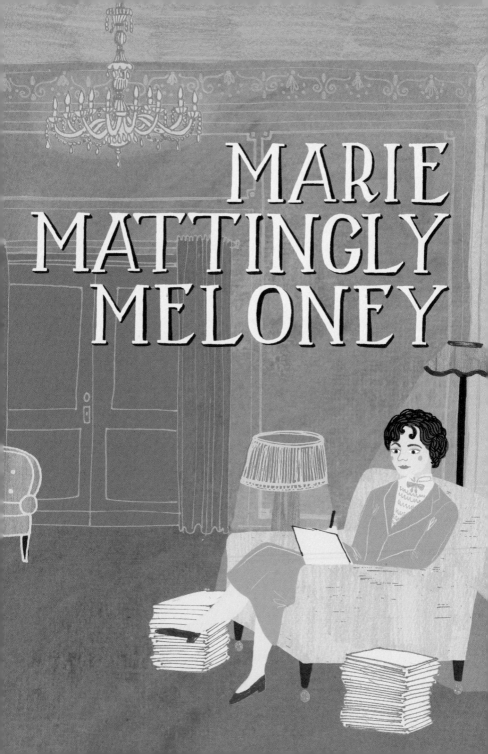

MARIE
MATTINGLY
MELONEY

MARIE MATTINGLY MELONEY was a driven, talented woman, who used her position as a journalist to be a positive force for good.

Educated partly by her editor mother, Marie landed a reporter job on the *Washington Post* at the age of sixteen, and at eighteen became chief of the *Denver Post's* Washington bureau. Marie was not only young, but small and frail; the sight of her covering heavyweight conventions and the Senate must have been arresting. Her first big scoop was the unannounced wedding of Admiral George Dewey, which she uncovered by chance.

When she was twenty-two, Marie moved to New York City, then deep in the smoky, liberating decadence of the Jazz Age. There she joined the staff of the *New York Sun*, *New York World*, followed by editing *Woman's Magazine* and then *The Delineator*. She was anything but an impartial, cold reporter: she would get involved in the causes she wrote about. Marie started a 'Better Homes in America' movement to improve conditions for those in cramped conditions and was way ahead of the curve on the nutrition debate, planning healthy eating campaigns and warning of the dangers of anorexia and obesity.

Marie was fearless. She interviewed Mussolini four times, and after Hitler broke their appointment for a meeting she turned him down when he tried to make another. She later went on to berate the Nazis for their banning of authors and book burning. At the age of fifty-nine, she was still working in publishing, albeit in the most glamorous of settings, editing *This Week* from her suite at the Waldorf Astoria hotel.

In 1920, Marie interviewed the 'pale, timid' Marie Skłodowska Curie for *The Delineator*. At the time, Curie was desperate to acquire more radium so she could continue to research its effects. Radium was incredibly expensive – $100,000 for just one gram – and Marie came away from the meeting having agreed to help raise the money. Within a year, after a whirlwind campaign that solicited many small donations from women across the country, the money had been raised. Curie was the recipient of her much-needed substance, presented to her in a lead-lined mahogany box. The two women became close friends, even meeting the president together, and Marie helped set up a book deal for Curie, which raised yet more money for her cause.

Cited as inspirational in *The Second Sex* by

NOT ONLY was Marie Curie the first woman to receive a Nobel Prize, she was the first to win it twice, and the only person so far to win in two different sciences – physics and chemistry.

Marie was born Maria Salomea Skłodowska into a poor family: her teacher parents had lost their money during Polish national uprisings. Her grandfather and father taught Marie and her four siblings at home. At ten, she went to school and did well, but was thwarted in her dream to attend a university in Poland because she was a woman. Marie worked hard as a governess to earn the money to go to Paris and continue her studies, all the time devouring information, revelling in the joy of learning.

Accepted to the Sorbonne to read physics and mathematics, Marie lived in a freezing garret, still tutoring, sometimes fainting through lack of food. She earned two degrees, and after graduating met Pierre Curie. They married in 1895 – Marie wore a dark navy dress, which would become her laboratory uniform – and the couple went on to have two children.

Marie and Pierre became a formidable team. They researched radioactive substances, coining the word 'radioactivity' and discovering two new elements – radium and polonium (named after Marie's home country). In 1903, along with Henri Becquerel, they were awarded the Nobel Prize in Physics for their work. Both Curies disliked publicity and felt awkward receiving money – they refused to take out patents on their discoveries because of their value to science and world health – but they eventually travelled to Stockholm to deliver the required lecture and be awarded the prize money, which they poured into research.

Tragedy struck in 1906 when Pierre was hit by a cart and died. Marie took over his physics chair at the University of Paris, where she went on to isolate radium, for which she won her Nobel Prize in Chemistry. This time, the Nobel Academy in Sweden were a little cooler about her coming to visit – Marie was at the centre of a scandal for having an affair with a married man, Paul Langevin.

During the First World War, Marie developed mobile radiography units for use on the battlefields, providing the radium from her personal supply. After the armistice, she received a stipend for more research from the government and toured the world giving lectures. Marie was ill with sickness contracted from her long-term exposure to radiation. In 1934, she died of aplastic anaemia. Her daughter and son-in-law received a Nobel Prize in Chemistry the following year.

In 1934, the year that Marie died, a maths student at Nanjing University was inspired by the great scientist to switch her major to physics. The student, Chien-Shiung Wu, went on to be christened 'the Chinese Marie Curie'. Like Marie, Chien-Shiung was modest and didn't seek out fame, preferring to let her research and achievements speak for themselves.

CHIEN-SHIUNG, OR 'courageous hero', more than lived up to her impressive name, making trips into the unknown to study and completing groundbreaking nuclear physics research.

Chien-Shiung was born at a turbulent time in China – just after the Xinhai Revolution, which overthrew the country's last imperial dynasty. Her teacher father encouraged her studies, and Chien's ability in maths and science shone. After studying in Nanjing, she set off in 1936 for America to study at the University of Michigan, but was lured to the University of California, San Francisco by its shiny

new particle accelerator. Chien completed her PhD there, and married fellow physicist Luke Chia-Liu Yuan, grandson of the first president of China.

Chien encountered much covert and overt racism and sexism. She missed China, struggled with English, and wore traditional qipao dresses under her lab coat. In addition, the Japanese invasion of her country in 1937 meant that she didn't hear from her family for eight years.

In March 1944, Chien joined the Manhattan Project at Columbia University, solving a crucial problem as the US raced to develop the first nuclear weapons.

After the Second World War, Chien was asked to stay on at Columbia University, where she worked on beta decay. She was detail-obsessed, which showed in her excellent results and was instrumental in her disproving the law of conservation of parity. Two of her colleagues went on to receive a Nobel Prize for their work in this area, but, controversially, Chien was overlooked for the honour. She did, however, go on to win accolades including the Wolf Prize and the Tom W. Bonner Prize.

Chien retired from Columbia but went on to work promoting girls in STEM (science, technology, engineering and maths) in the US and China.

Many have attributed to sexism the Swedish Academy's decision to overlook Chien's work when awarding the Nobel Prize. Such accusations have dogged the award. Fellow nuclear researcher Lise Meitner – whose pioneering research in Germany worried President Roosevelt so much that it led directly to the establishment of the Manhattan Project – also missed out on a medal in 1944, when her co-researcher Otto Hahn gained his chemistry prize.

LISE

109
Mt

MEITNER

$^{92}_{36}Kr$

$3 ^1_0 n$

$^{141}_{56}Ba$

MARIE CURIE

was her counterpart – she was described by Albert Einstein as the German version

Had to flee occupied Europe to escape the Nazis, as did

DESPITE LISE Meitner's research playing a direct part in the creation of the atomic bomb, she was known as the scientist who, according to her tombstone, 'never lost her humanity'.

Born in Vienna, Austria into a supportive, affluent family, Lise became only the second woman to gain a degree in physics from the city's university. She then went on to Germany to study in Berlin, where physicist Max Planck let her attend his lectures and hired her as an assistant. It was here that she met scientist Otto Hahn, and they became collaborators. The pair moved into the brand-new Kaiser Wilhelm Institute for Chemistry, although Lise was unpaid and had to work in a broom cupboard until she threatened to leave for another job.

In 1917, she and Otto discovered protactinium, and Lise was given her own physics section at the institute. In 1926, she would become the first German woman to be made a full professor of physics. For thirty years, Lise and Otto would scramble to uncover 'heavy' elements – the early stages of the discovery of nuclear power.

Lise was Jewish, and the tide of anti-Semitism was rising. In 1938, at the age of sixty, she was forced to tear herself away from cutting-edge research and flee Germany for Sweden with only a few basic possessions. She corresponded with Otto, and they continued their research together – as far as Lise was concerned, she was still part of the team.

Lise began working with her nephew, Otto Frisch, and together they articulated an explanation for the radiochemical process that Hahn and collaborator Fritz Strassman had discovered, calling it

ELSA SCHIAPARELLI

CLAUDE CAHUN

LEONORA CARRINGTON

'nuclear fission'. The discovery would go on to power whole countries, as well as being used in bombs.

Lise latterly refused an offer from America to work on the weapon-researching Manhattan Project and was rueful about Hiroshima, saying she was 'sorry that the bomb had to be invented'.

Otto Hahn won the 1944 Nobel Prize in Chemistry for his work in discovering nuclear fission. The deliberations of the committee were eventually released in 1999, when it became apparent that Lise's contributions were overlooked due to bias, ignorance and Lise's hurried relocation. At the time Lise was angry at her passing over for the prize, but, although the relationship had a few bumps, she remained friends with Otto. In 1997, twenty-nine years after her death, she had an element named after her: meitnerium.

After her relocation to Stockholm, Lise occasionally travelled to Copenhagen, where she collaborated with fellow nuclear experimenter Niels Bohr at his institute. In fact, it was Niels who spread the word about nuclear fission to the USA, stealing Meitner and Frisch's thunder a little.

In 1943, Niels was also forced to escape to Sweden. A 2013 biography of film star Greta Garbo claimed that the film star had intervened personally by calling King Gustav V to help Niels flee Denmark. In the book, Garbo was also credited with having identified Nazi collaborators in Stockholm. Others maintain that the work was done by another spy who used her name as an alias. However, given her incredible life story, Swedish roots and secretive nature, the seemingly fantastical tale could well be true.

ETHEREAL YET assertive, Greta Garbo was an exotic, European antidote to cookie-cutter American actresses. Her 'I want to be alone' catchphrase resonated through her real life – she hated the trappings of stardom.

Greta Lovisa Gustafsson was born into a poor family in Sweden. Her icy-sharp beauty was first noticed when she was picked to appear in film adverts while working in sales for a Swedish department store. This resulted in a role in a film, which, in turn, led Greta to theatre school. When director Mauritz Stiller cast her in *The Saga of Gösta Berling*, the two began a partnership that would take her to the USA.

Greta's huge break came when Louis B. Mayer of MGM studios came looking for European talent. Mauritz and Greta met him in Berlin, and he signed them both to a deal. Shortly afterwards, the pair travelled by boat to America. It took six months for Greta to even get a screen test, but the results were immediate: after a makeover and elocution lessons, the luminous star was ready for her close-up.

And what a close-up. Greta was the master of conveying complex emotions through the smallest of expressions. Her first film, *Torrent*, was a hit, and there followed a string of vampish, erotically charged roles that established her as a silent-film legend. Already, however, her secretive, reclusive nature was starting to emerge – she asked for screens to hide behind while filming emotional scenes.

Unlike many of her squeakily voiced contemporaries, Greta survived the leap to talkies with ease, making thirteen

more films for MGM. She was nominated four times for Academy Awards, but never attended a ceremony. Even when she won an honorary award, she didn't appear. She hated parties, never signed autographs and disliked crowds. She made her last film, *Two-Faced Woman*, at thirty-six, retired to Manhattan, New York and died at eighty-four.

Greta chose to live alone for most of her life; she never married or had a partner. Her relationship with actor John Gilbert in the 1920s was her biggest romance. However, she had affairs: conductor Leopold Stokowski, film star Louise Brooks, photographer Cecil Beaton and Russian millionaire George Schlee. She also had a long and passionate relationship with writer Mercedes de Acosta, with whom she was friends for thirty years.

KATHERINE HEPBURN

...and Greta enjoyed jogging together in their seventies

Greta Garbo

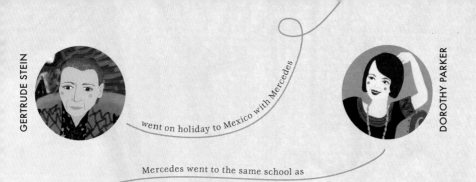

EMBRACING IDEAS at least forty years ahead of her time, but often airily dismissed by her contemporaries, Mercedes de Acosta was an out and proud lesbian, a vegetarian who refused to wear furs, a prominent suffragist and a student of Eastern philosophies and religion.

Born in New York to a family of Cuban American socialites, Mercedes went to school in Manhattan with Dorothy Parker. Even as a child, she was a striking sight – she dressed as a boy until she was seven. When she was five, theatre manager Augustin Daly spotted her in Saint Patrick's Cathedral and offered to adopt her on the spot.

At the age of twenty-six Mercedes published a book of poetry, *Moods*, with two further collections, almost a dozen plays (of which only four were actually produced) and one novel to follow. But it is for her love affairs that she is best known. As her friend Alice B. Toklas said, 'Say what you will about Mercedes, she's had the most important women of the twentieth century.'

Mercedes' list of lovers reads like the most glamorous Hollywood pool party: Eva Le Gallienne, Alla Nazimova, Marlene Dietrich. Mercedes made lesbianism chic, modern and aspirational. She cut an impressive figure as a proto-goth, striding the streets of Manhattan in trousers, pointed shoes with buckles, a tricorn hat and cape, her face white, lips red and shiny black hair slicked back. Tallulah Bankhead called her Countess Dracula.

At the age of thirty-eight, Mercedes met Greta Garbo, with whom she fell deeply in love. Their twelve-year relationship was tempestuous and rocky. The two spent a lot of time together, but Greta later shut the 'obsessed' Mercedes down, sending her letters begging to be left alone. Greta was reportedly terrified that Mercedes would expose her private life.

In the 1930s, Mercedes became friends with an Indian mystic, Meher Baba, and she developed a deep interest in Hindu philosophies. She practised yoga and travelled to India to meet the Maharishi.

Towards the end of her life, Mercedes fell ill and was forced to sell her diamonds to pay her medical bills. She also wrote a fundraising, tell-all autobiography that lost her many friends. Nevertheless, she retained an impish zeal that enchanted many, including Andy Warhol.

One of Mercedes' longest-running romances was with the dancer Isadora Duncan, whom she met in 1917 in New York, and who wrote a passionate, unashamedly sensual poem that extolled the virtues of her 'Arch Angel's' 'slender hips' and 'secret place'.

A GLORIOUSLY eccentric free spirit, Isadora Duncan brought joy to the world of dance and revelled in a bohemian life.

Born in San Francisco, this precocious prancer had set up neighbourhood dance classes by the age of six. Isadora's approach to dance was free-form – she'd had no formal training, preferring to interpret the music with feeling and improvise – and her trademark moves were running and leaping. She left home in her teens, moving to Chicago, Illinois then New York. Due to her unconventional way of dancing, however, she found it hard to get ballet or theatre work.

Yearning for European culture, Isadora travelled to London in 1898. She studied Greek mythology and wandered around the statues of the British Museum for inspiration. Informed by nature and ancient rituals, she rejected the conventions of ballet, calling for its abolition, and performed barefoot in tunics and togas, wrapped in scarves.

Still not accepted by the dance establishment, Isadora performed in private houses, but her break came when fellow modern dancer Loie Fuller took her on tour around Europe.

Isadora had two children, a daughter by theatre designer Gordon Craig, and a son by sewing machine heir Paris Singer. Tragedy struck in 1913, however, as the siblings drowned when the car they and their nanny were in drove into the Seine.

Isadora poured her heart into her work. The success of her shows meant she could open dance schools. The first, in Germany, spawned six 'Isadorables': pupils who were all adopted by Isadora.

Isadora was bisexual, an atheist and a fervent communist. In 1921, she moved

to Russia, where she met and had a brief marriage to poet Sergey Aleksandrovich Yesenin. Two years after their split, he committed suicide.

Isadora's final years were to be an emotional struggle. She was often drunk, had a series of very public love affairs and led a transient lifestyle in France. She died at the age of fifty when her long, trailing silk scarf got caught in the wheels of her open-top car.

On hearing of Isadora's death, the writer Gertrude Stein somewhat callously commented, 'Affectations can be dangerous.' The two had both grown up in Oakland, California, in the 1880s, but met in the salons and drawing rooms of Europe. Gertrude immortalised Isadora in a pen portrait, 'Orta or One Dancing', a fluid, repetitive written piece that echoes and gives meaning to Isadora's flowing, unique movements.

TAMARA ROJO

Portrays her in Five Brahms Waltzes in the Manner of Isadora Duncan

COCO CHANEL

SYLVIA BEACH

GEORGIA O'KEEFFE

Her poetry inspired

A CHAMPION of modernism, with a magnetic personality, writer Gertrude Stein was an avid collector — of art and of people.

Gertrude grew up in Europe and Oakland, California. Her family were wealthy, and she was particularly close to her brother. Her mother and father died while she was in her teens, so she was sent to live with her uncle in Baltimore, Maryland. She was bright, graduating from Radcliffe College, where she conducted experiments that foreshadowed her stream-of-consciousness writing style. She then studied medicine at Johns Hopkins, where she clashed with teachers over her liberal views and left before graduation.

Gertrude, her partner Alice B. Toklas and brother Leo moved to France, where they set up home together and started to collect art. The high walls of their Paris apartment were hung thick with brightly coloured modern paintings – Cézanne, Gauguin, Renoir, Picasso, Matisse, Toulouse-Lautrec. Consequently, for many decades, their home became a hub for emerging artists and writers – on any given Saturday night, you might find Henri Matisse, Ezra Pound, Pablo Picasso, F. Scott Fitzgerald, James Joyce and Ernest Hemingway gathered, discussing art and literature. In 1914, partly because of her intense relationship with Alice, Gertrude 'split' with her brother and they divided the collection, barely speaking again.

Gertrude's literary career is almost secondary to her social life and patronage of arts, but her modernist, free-flowing

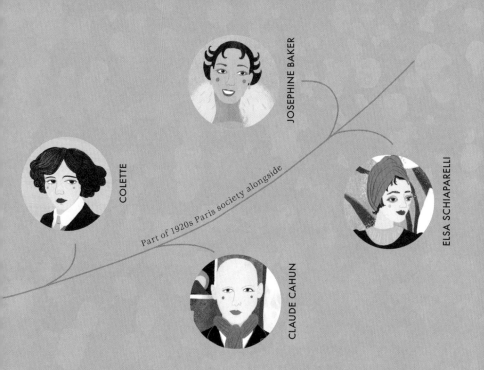

JOSEPHINE BAKER

COLETTE

ELSA SCHIAPARELLI

Part of 1920s Paris society alongside

CLAUDE CAHUN

poetry was published from 1909. Her only commercial success, however, was *The Autobiography of Alice B. Toklas.*

During the First World War, Gertrude and Alice drove ambulances alongside Ernest Hemingway and E.E. Cummings. In 1934, she embarked on a lecture tour of the USA and continued to host events for artists and writers in her Paris apartment. She would do so up until her death at the age of seventy-two.

Part of the Paris set alongside Gertrude Stein was bookshop owner and publisher Sylvia Beach. Stein was a customer of Sylvia's bookshop, Shakespeare and Company, and Sylvia attended Stein's salons. Sylvia's shop served as another hub for the crème de la crème of romantic, inter-war literary Paris. It was an era in which artists, poets and philosophers

thronged the streets of the Left Bank, collaborating, deliberating and revelling in the joy of their art. Sylvia Beach wrote about Stein and Toklas in her book Shakespeare and Company, a memoir of that Paris. 'Gertrude Stein had so much charm,' she once said, 'that she could often, though not always, get away with the most monstrous absurdities, which she uttered with a certain childish malice.'

BEACH'S LIFE reads almost like a real-life romantic fiction novel. Girl moves to Paris, falls in love, opens a bookshop. Girl publishes one of the most controversial novels in the English language. We did say almost.

Sylvia's family was religious: she was born in a parsonage, and her father was descended from a long line of vicars in Maryland. The whole family was in love with France, and they spent long stints in Paris. Sylvia herself adored Europe, and returned to live in Spain. On the outbreak of the First World War, she volunteered for the Red Cross there, with whom she served in the Balkans.

Sylvia was back in Paris, studying literature, when she made a field trip to La Maison des Amis des Livres, a bookshop and free lending library that specialised in modern French literature, run by twenty-three-year-old Adrienne Monnier. Sylvia was inspired both by Monnier – the pair became lovers – and her La Maison. Not having the funds to open a French bookshop in the USA, she decided to open a Paris bookshop that sold English books: Shakespeare and Company.

It was a dreamy place — overstuffed armchairs, piles of books, sunlight streaming through windows. Writers gathered here, drawn by Sylvia's nurturing kindness. She lent money to those struggling and kept a bed in a backroom for those without shelter.

Henry Miller, accompanied by his lover and editor Anaïs Nin, brought in a draft of *Tropic of Cancer*, while, less convivially, Ernest Hemingway once punched a vase of tulips over a stack of new books after reading an unfavourable article about him titled, 'The Dumb Ox'.

SYLVIA BEACH

The store held regular literary readings that attracted the likes of André Breton and James Joyce. Joyce became a good friend of Adrienne and Sylvia, and when he couldn't find a publisher for his controversial *Ulysses*, Beach stepped in and put it out herself.

The bookshop shut when German troops invaded Paris. Sylvia, who had moved out of Adrienne's apartment by then, spent six months in an internment camp for employing a Jewish assistant, emerging after the liberation. Adrienne and Sylvia were still friends, but not lovers, and spent much time together until Adrienne's suicide in 1955. A year later, Sylvia wrote her memoir, *Shakespeare and Company*. She died in Paris in 1962.

Two attendees at Sylvia's salons, and close friends of her and Monnier, were Claude Cahun and Marcel Moore,

stepsisters and lovers. Photographer Claude had taken a picture of Sylvia when her shop opened, and it is thought that she may have sometimes worked at Shakespeare and Company. She was certainly owner of a registration card for the store.

SIMONE DE BEAUVOIR

was her good friend

WAY AHEAD of its time, Claude Cahun's surreal art is firmly fixated on Claude Cahun. But if you were a Jewish, Marxist lesbian in love with your stepsister in the early twentieth century, your art would probably be surreal and self-reflective too.

Claude Cahun was born Lucy Schwob in France into a family beset by mental illness. She went to school in the south of England, then on to the Sorbonne. During her teens, her father remarried, and Claude found herself sharing a house with Suzanne Malherbe, later to become Marcel Moore. The two girls were immediately obsessed with each other; it was to become a lifelong love. Claude was non-binary, or 'neuter' as she described it: 'Shuffle the cards. Masculine? Feminine? It depends on the situation.'

Claude and Marcel were more than lovers — they were everything to each other. They held Paris salons together and collaborated on their art. Cahun was primarily known as a writer during her life, but her visual work is her true legacy. She bound the aesthetics of surrealism to narcissistic self-portraits, where she'd take on different personas: a circus strongman, a little girl with hair in ribbons, a vampire, a Japanese puppet.

Claude and Marcel's art was on the very fringes of the mainstream – they exhibited in the surrealist show at Galerie Ratton in 1936 but they didn't get the publicity accorded to others, which frustrated them. In 1937, the stepsisters upped and moved to Jersey. They continued creating art, but the shadow of war engulfed the island in 1940, with the invasion of the Nazis, and the pair's focus turned to resistance.

Claude and Marcel's self-contained resistance movement went beyond art to politics. They branded themselves 'Der Soldat Ohne Namen', 'The Soldier Without a Name', and created inflammatory flyers and collages. Then, disguised as little old ladies, they left their propaganda in the pockets of soldiers and in cigarette packets, and tossed it through staff-car windows. In 1944, they were caught and arrested, and sentenced to death. Luckily liberation was around the corner. In 1945 they were released. Claude died in 1954.

The high point of Claude's career was exhibiting some heavily symbolic objects in the Exposition Surréaliste d'Objèts show at Galerie Ratton in 1936. Also in attendance was Salvador Dalí, a friend and surrealist compadre of Claude's who mixed in the same circles. Like Claude, Dalí was also a keen collaborator, deeply inspired by his muse Gala Dalí, about whom he once said, 'It is mostly with your blood, Gala, that I paint my pictures.'

A WILD muse, romantic adventurer and canny publicist, Gala's mystery and magnetism inspired some of the world's finest painters and writers.

Born Elena Ivanovna Diakonova, Gala grew up in Moscow, becoming a teacher. On contracting tuberculosis, she was treated in Switzerland, where she met budding poet Paul Éluard. He nicknamed Elena 'Gala', from the French word meaning 'triumph' or 'festival'. The book-obsessed pair decamped to Paris, married and had a daughter, although Gala didn't enjoy motherhood. Paul introduced Gala to some of the leading lights of the surrealist movement, but her artistic interest in the group developed into lust, and in 1922 she started a two-year affair with painter Max Ernst.

In 1929, Gala and Paul spent the summer with an emerging painter, Salvador Dalí. For Gala and Salvador – ten years her junior – it was love at first sight. The pair married in 1934 and remained together until Gala's death. Their relationship, however, was anything but exclusive.

That Salvador and Gala were deeply in love is indisputable. He fed off her for his work – most notably in the iconic *Galarina*, in which Gala appeared bare-breasted. He signed her name alongside his on paintings, and created a set of symbols that represented their initials. He also described how Gala acted as his agent. But Salvador had a complex sexual make-up. He was repulsed by female genitalia, a virgin when he met Gala, and was turned on by watching his lover with others. Gala, with her high sex drive, indulged him with gusto. She had a string of affairs with young artists and continued to sleep with her ex-husband Paul.

In 1968, Salvador bought Gala a castle, Púbol, in Girona, which became Gala's summer home. She banned Salvador from visiting and, even in her late seventies, entertained lithe young lovers by a pool decorated with busts of Richard Wagner.

Gala and Salvador's relationship became more strained. His retirement frustrated him and he grew less tolerant of Gala's affairs, eventually assaulting her and breaking her hip — a sadly bitter ending to a great love story. Gala died of flu in 1982 and was buried in the grounds of her beloved castle.

One of Salvador's closest collaborators was the designer Elsa Schiaparelli. The Italian couturier used Dalí's design to produce the 'lobster dress' – a gown printed with a large crustacean. She also worked with him to create a headpiece shaped like a high-heeled slipper – the 'shoe hat' – which Gala ended up keeping, and the 'tears dress', a gown printed to give the illusion of savagely ripped and flayed flesh.

Designed clothes for

GRETA GARBO

ONE OF the boldest fashion designers of all time, Elsa Schiaparelli created bravely original couture that was more art than clothing.

Elsa came from an aristocratic, scholarly background; however, she hated the rarefied atmosphere of her home in Rome and, at the age of twenty-two, fled to a childcare job in London to avoid marrying a parentally approved Russian aristocrat. A year later, she married Polish-Swiss fraudulent 'mystic' Willem de Wendt, with whom she had a child, the wonderfully nicknamed Gogo. The pair separated within six years.

After a short time in New York, in 1922 Elsa moved to Paris and started experimenting with clothes design. Although she wasn't trained, her artistic skill and eye for modernity gave her clothes an edge. She opened her own fashion house in 1927, and her career took off with a collection of knitwear emblazoned with surreal images.

Elsa's sharp wit made her the darling of the Parisian artistic social scene, and she brought that same humour to her designs. However, Elsa's attention-grabbing pieces often result in her more practical contributions to fashion being overlooked – she pioneered the wrap dress and visible zips, and used innovative synthetic textiles.

But it was in the olfactory realm that Elsa reigned supreme. Her Shocking de Schiaparelli perfume came in a bottle inspired by Mae West's shape and Dalí's paintings, all in Elsa's signature bright pink packaging. Her flair for marketing contributed to its instant global success.

In 1941, with the spectre of Nazism creeping nearer, Elsa moved to New York, where she volunteered as a nurse. She returned to Paris at the end of the occupation, but the world was irreparably darker and her frivolous designs were eclipsed by the new practicality of work from couturiers such as Christian Dior. The House of Schiaparelli went bankrupt in 1954. Elsa spent much of her retirement in Tunisia, dying in Paris at the age of eighty-three.

It would be another fifty years before Italian designer Miuccia Prada started work at her grandfather's luggage company. But the two women had much in common. Both of them collaborated with artists and worked with intelligence and wit on the catwalk. Both played with, parodied and subverted feminine conventions. There were even echoes of Schiaparelli in Prada's work – lips, insects crawling over dresses, experimentation with fabric. In 2012, the pair were commemorated in an exhibition, 'Impossible Conversations', at the Metropolitan Museum of Art's Costume Institute in New York, which gave the effect of the two being in conversation with each other about subjects such as art, politics and women.

A MIME student, a member of the Communist party and a women's rights activist with a PhD in social science, Miuccia doesn't come from a traditional fashion designer background. It's perhaps these unusual influences that make her designs so groundbreaking, and have helped her amass a personal fortune of over $11 billion.

Miuccia was twenty-nine when she met her future husband and business partner Patrizio Bertelli and entered her family's luxury leather bag business. She gave the traditional company a shake-up, and in 1985 added modern black nylon backpacks to the range, which became a cult success.

Debuting her womenswear line in 1988, Miuccia's style contrasted with that of most Italian designers – she brought a modernism to her collections, making clothes that were defiantly 'unpretty', cerebral and practical. Her second line, Miu Miu (after her nickname), was introduced in 1992, and menswear in 1995. Miuccia's business sense and strong aesthetic, combined with a series of wise acquisitions to form a business portfolio, made for continuing financial success. She has, however, never lost her sense of impish fun – on good days she's known to shoot out of her office on a slide installed by artist Carsten Höller.

Since 1993 and the opening of her contemporary art foundation, Miuccia's love of all things artistic has come to the fore. She has exhibited works by Anish

Kapoor, Louise Bourgeois and Sam Taylor-Wood, and established a museum in Milan, open to the public, designed by Dutch architect Rem Koolhaas.

German designer Jil Sander shares a minimalist aesthetic and love of high-tech fabrics with Miuccia. Sander's work and personal style are very clearly influenced by early Prada collections. Miuccia obviously admired Jil, and in 1999 she bought a controlling share in her company. Though the business relationship has been fraught – Jil left three times and returned twice – Miuccia sold the company in 2006, in better financial shape than when it was purchased.

COCO CHANEL

and the simple 'little black dress' inspired her

MIUCCIA PRADA

KNOWN AS the 'queen of less' for her pared-down approach to design, Jil Sander's strong signature look and minimalist style has made for a sterling career in fashion.

Even as a child, Jil knew her aesthetic well. Despite her teacher's disapproval, she'd wear trousers to school with home-made corduroy shirts, hand-sewn by her mother. Jil used the same sewing machine when she set up her own label at the age of twenty-four.

Jil gave herself a good grounding in the industry, studying textiles at home in Germany and at the University of California. She went on to write for fashion magazines in New York, but returned to Germany when she was twenty-one, on the death of her father.

Jil's first collection in her own name combined clean lines, avoided bright colours and print, and used accessories very sparingly. Her silhouettes were borrowed from menswear, and she made the practical decision early on to create mainly separates, which could be combined for different looks and occasions. She wasn't bent or swayed

by trends, but offered a more timeless look to a loyal, affluent fan base. By the late 1980s, the label was flourishing, and Jil's clothing was stocked around the world.

In 1999, Jil sold 75 per cent of her company to Prada, but remained as creative designer and chairwoman. She clashed with Prada's CEO Patrizio Bertelli, and resigned in 2000, along with most of her creative staff. She returned in 2003, but by the next year had resigned again. She went to work for Japanese high street brand Uniqlo, creating a utilitarian womens- and menswear collection called J+, which she produced until 2011. In 2012, she returned once more to her namesake brand, only to resign again in 2013.

Jil Sander is an admirer of Coco Chanel — another fan of a simple, unified look, who paired the functional with the beautiful and once said,'Before you leave the house, look in the mirror and take one thing off.' Like Jil, Coco also appropriated traditionally masculine shapes, and opted for sophistication and hidden luxury over ostentation.

JIL
SANDER

COCO CHANEL brought a hatpin-sharp brain to fashion, transforming the way women dressed, smelled and moved.

Gabrielle 'Coco' Chanel was born illegitimately into a poor family. Her parents and four brothers and sisters lived in a one-bedroom flat in Brive-la-Gaillarde in France. Coco's mother died when she was twelve, and she and her sisters were sent to a strict convent school, where Coco learned to sew. On leaving school, she sang in cabaret and was noticed by rich textile heir Étienne Balsan, who elevated the lip-bitingly witty Coco into the most decadent of circles. She then moved on to another lover, Arthur Capel, the Englishman who would go on to finance her line of clothes. These were designed in innovative fabrics such as jersey and tricot, and sold in her own shops in Deauville, Biarritz and Paris. By 1916, Coco's success was such that she was able to pay Arthur back. Three years later, she became a registered Parisian couturière.

During the 1920s, the house of Chanel revolutionised fashion, dressing women for dancing, flirting, driving cars and working. Coco pioneered the now ubiquitous bias cut, the spaghetti-string shoulder strap, the long, floating evening scarf, the Breton shirt, the collarless cardigan jacket, the boyish haircut, suntans, costume jewellery and, most famously, the little black dress. Her fashion empire expanded, and by 1927 she owned five properties on the same street in Paris. Coco's perfume, Chanel No 5, was a worldwide sensation. After licensing her brand name to Pierre and Paul Wertheimer, however, she had to fight to regain control of her product.

Coco's lifestyle was reckless and outré – she loved cocaine and morphine, and she had a series of aristocratic and influential lovers. During the Second World War, Chanel picked her romantic partner unwisely, having a liaison with Nazi officer Hans Günther von Dincklage. Her behaviour during the war was equally dubious; at best she was ambivalent towards the Germans. It's thought that an intervention from Winston Churchill meant Coco was found not guilty on the count of collaboration by the Free French purge committee. Her cause may have been helped by information she had on very high-level British Nazi sympathisers.

A cooling-off period in Switzerland ensued. Then, in 1954, at the age of seventy, Coco resumed her fashion career in France, where her star ascended once more. At her funeral in 1971, many of the mourners wore Chanel suits.

The writer Colette moved in the same Parisian social circles as Coco. She sold Coco a summer-house – after a tough transaction. Chanel described Colette as a 'highly intelligent woman', and said, 'The only two female writers who appeal to me are Madame de Noailles and Colette.' In return, Colette described Coco: 'If every human face bears a resemblance to some animal, then Mademoiselle Chanel is a small black bull.'

INDULGENTLY SENSUAL in both her writing and life, Colette shocked, thrilled and documented the Paris demi-monde.

Brought up in rural Burgundy, Sidonie-Gabrielle Colette was raised with a blend of lyrical beauty and hard-living realness that set the pattern for the rest of her life.

At the age of twenty, she was swept off her feet by writer, critic and sexual experimenter Henry 'Willy' Gauthier-Villars, thirteen years her senior. He took her to Paris, to decadent parties and intellectual salons, then locked her in a room and made her write. She produced four books — the 'Claudine' series, a semi-autobiographical tale, peppered with salacious sapphic seduction. He published these under his name. Consequently, when the pair parted ways Colette got no royalties, and so supported herself touring the music halls of France, playing Claudine. During this period, she had an affair with 'Missy', the Marquise de Belbeuf, who dressed in men's clothes.

Drawing again on her own experiences, Colette published *The Vagabond*, about a divorcee-turned-actress, which was received well by critics and established her career. In 1912, she married Henry de Jouvenel, who was the editor of *Le Matin*, a magazine to which she contributed. The pair had a daughter, Colette de Jouvenel, or Bel-Gazou. Colette's marriage enabled her to devote more time to writing, and in 1920 she published *Chéri*, the story of a woman who has an affair with a much younger man. Perhaps it was autobiographical – in 1924, after an affair with her sixteen-year-old stepson, she split with her husband.

In 1935, Colette married Maurice Goudeket, her partner for the rest of her career. Her best-known work, *Gigi*, was published late in life – at seventy-one. It tells the story of a young courtesan who marries, rather than seduces, her wealthy lover. It was adapted into a play in 1951, starring a young Audrey Hepburn, and then a film in 1958 that starred Leslie Caron. Colette died at the age of eighty-one, becoming the first woman to receive a state funeral in France.

As a young student, fellow French writer Simone de Beauvoir would rummage through Parisian bookshops looking for Colette's novels which de Beauvoir admired for their insights into female psychology. She acknowledged them in her own work: *The Second Sex* contains twenty-two references to Colette's work.

AUDREY HEPBURN

GERTRUDE STEIN

starred in the broadway production of her book Gigi

was one of her good friends

SIMONE DE

ISADORA DUNCAN

GERTRUDE STEIN

The Second Sex cites inspirational women including

MARIE CURIE

FIERCELY INTELLECTUAL, writer and pioneering feminist Simone de Beauvoir lived her philosophies to the letter.

As a girl, Simone was devoutly religious, even contemplating becoming a nun. Her family was bourgeois but in a precarious financial situation, so encouraged Simone's education to ensure her security. Simone was precociously clever, studying maths and literature at school, then going on to the Sorbonne to soak up philosophy. During this time, she met fellow deep-thinking students Claude Lévi-Strauss, Maurice Merleau-Ponty and Jean-Paul Sartre, with whom she

fell in love. Jean-Paul and Simone never married, but they would remain together until his death in 1980. They had an open relationship: Simone was a teacher at the Lycée Molière and had affairs with her students, sometimes introducing them to Jean-Paul to create complicated love-triangles. The pair went on to have affairs throughout their lives, but always returned to and supported each other.

Alongside their intricate love life, Jean-Paul and Simone's professional lives cross-pollinated. They whispered in jazz clubs and in cafés about their existentialist philosophies. Simone wrote essays and

SYLVIA BEACH

was one of her friends

INDIRA GANDHI

It Changed My Life includes an encounter between Simone and

books, culminating in her major work, *The Second Sex*, which draws brilliantly on philosophy, psychology and literature to describe and analyse the treatment of women through history. From it comes her infamous quote: 'One is not born, but rather becomes, a woman.'

Simone and Jean-Paul's influence hung over the 1950s and 1960s like a pall of Gauloises cigarette smoke: they practically invented the existential beatnik. As she matured, Simone grew fascinated with ageing, which became a theme of her later work. She was also a prime mover in the French feminist movement, writing and signing the Manifesto of the 343 in 1971, which was signed by 343 famous women who'd had abortions (then illegal) in France. Simone died in Paris at seventy-eight, six years after Jean-Paul.

Fellow philosopher and writer Iris Murdoch also wrote more novels than works of philosophy. Iris was an ardent fan of de Beauvoir, and spoke of her 'admiration', describing Simone's *The Mandarins* as 'a remarkable book, a novel on the grand scale, courageous in its exactitude and endearing because of its persistent seriousness'.

THROUGH HER novels, Iris Murdoch pulled apart and examined the mind, laying bare the intricacies of human consciousness and love in an inventive, gripping way.

Born in Dublin, Ireland, Iris had a happy childhood as an only child who loved singing. Her parents sent her to progressive private schools, and then to Oxford University, where she studied the greats and philosophy, and joined the Communist party. While there, she also met her friend Philippa Foot, a fellow philosopher, with whom she lived until after the Second World War.

During the war, Iris worked with the United Nations Relief and Rehabilitation Administration, heading to Belgium and Austria, where she worked in camps with refugees. After the war, she was awarded a fellowship and teaching post at Oxford's St Anne's College, where she remained until 1963. During this time, she met and married John Bayley, a novelist and English professor. Theirs was a curious relationship – he disliked sex and she had numerous affairs with men and women.

Iris' first book, *Under the Net*, was published in 1954, and went on to be one of her most popular. She would produce twenty-five more novels, the most famous of which, *The Sea, the Sea* (an introspective examination of the obsessions of a playwright and director),

IRIS

won the 1978 Booker Prize. In 1987, she was made a Dame of the British Empire.

Iris was diagnosed with Alzheimer's disease in 1995. She spent the last two years of her life cared for by John.

While at Badminton school, Iris befriended another homesick girl, who she described as frail and delicate and anxious to fit in. That girl was Indira Gandhi, who went on to become the prime minister of India. The pair would later meet again at Somerville College, Oxford University. After Indira's death, Iris flew to New Delhi to make a speech at a conference that commemorated the politician's life.

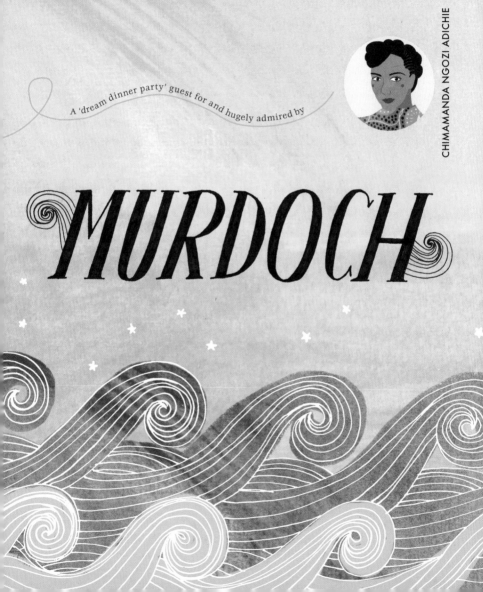

A 'dream dinner party' guest for and hugely admired by

CHIMAMANDA NGOZI ADICHIE

MURDOCH

Had a meeting with

KNOWN AS 'Mother India', Indira Gandhi was a major figure in the Indian independence movement.

The only daughter of India's first prime minister, Jawaharlal Nehru, and the granddaughter of Motilal Nehru, one of the independence movement's pioneers, Indira was brought up in Allahabad and in Switzerland.

When she was twenty-four, she married Feroze Gandhi, a fellow Congress party member. The pair had two children, although Indira and Feroze lived separate lives for most of their marriage. After her mother's death, Indira acted as her father's assistant, getting the best on-the-job training in politics available. Her role broadened when her father came to power in 1947, and in 1959 she was elected party president. She was made minister of information and broadcasting by her father's successor, Lal Bahadur Shastri. On his death in 1966, she became prime minister.

Indira's first years in the job were rocky: the party was split, it lost its majority, and Indira was accused of being its grandees' puppet. In 1971, she ran for power with the slogan 'garibi hatao', or 'eradicate poverty', aiming to unite castes and classes.

India was now self-sufficient in food production and this, combined with winning the 1971 war in Pakistan and the creation of Bangladesh, sent Indira's popularity soaring. After serving three terms, however, her authoritarian policies, a conviction for electoral malpractice and the declaration of a state of emergency saw voters turning against her. She was accused of running a dictatorship propped up by her son, Sanjay, and lost the election in 1977, but returned to power in 1980.

Sanjay's death in a plane crash in 1980 rocked Indira. The country was in turmoil: Sikhs in the Punjab were demanding an autonomous state and had occupied the holy Golden Temple, so Indira sent in troops, killing hundreds of people. In October 1984, in retaliation, Indira was shot and killed by two of her bodyguards.

Some of Indira's happiest times were spent in Shantiniketan, at a school run around simple principles by the poet Rabindranath Tagore. The school was visited a few years after Indira's time there by educationalist Maria Montessori, and it helped form her thinking about 'cosmic education'. Maria also met Indira's father, Jawaharlal Nehru. The trip was a success, and resulted in Maria training over a thousand Indian teachers – her movement continues to be incredibly popular in the country.

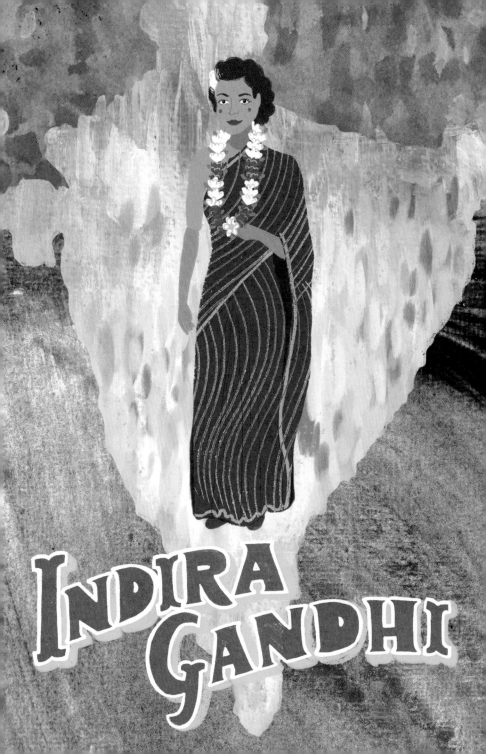

MARIA MONTESSORI'S radical educational methods built on the way children naturally learn. Her ability to combine a highly rational way of thinking with her desire to promote peace and love created a blueprint for progressive schools across the globe.

From an early age, Maria was bright and determined, and would not be limited by her sex. Set on a career in engineering, she attended an all-boys institute to achieve her goal. She later realised she wanted to be a doctor and applied to the University of Rome, where she eventually gained admittance.

Maria's time at university was harsh — she was harassed and suffered penalties for being a woman. She persisted, however, and became one of the first women in Italy to become a doctor of medicine. She also had an illegitimate child, Mario, whom she had to put into foster care in order to continue working as a doctor. He would later become her research assistant.

Maria worked with children with learning disabilities, forming a nascent educational philosophy, making speeches and writing papers. After completing a philosophy degree with a heavy element of psychology, she took over the care and education of a nursery for low-income families in Rome. She used the school as a model for her future establishments: equipment was child-sized, there were exercises to be done, children learned practical home-making skills, and

classrooms were open-plan and airy. The children were treated as individuals and given free choice and responsibility. The school was an instant success. More opened, and Maria's methods were employed across the region. She soon became a full-time educational expert, travelling around the world. Her Montessori schools were an international phenomenon.

Women's rights were also paramount to Maria – she was an ardent campaigner for them, both in Italy and around the world. In 1934, with the rise of Benito Mussolini, who was strongly opposed to her promotion of peace through education, Maria took her son and left her country. They lived in Barcelona, England and Holland, eventually settling for a period in India.

Maria's final years were spent in Amsterdam, and touring Europe and India. By now she was the grande dame of education, being nominated for a Nobel Peace Prize six times, and winning countless other medals and awards. She died in Holland at the age of eighty-one.

Maria's educational methods helped create a generation of bright minds across Europe, including an attendee at one of Maria's schools in Amsterdam: Anne Frank. Anne's parents decided that a Montessori education would suit her as she was so stubborn and talkative. Her teachers remembered Anne as a girl who loved being in plays and was always full of sparky ideas.

ONE OF the most famous teenagers in history, Anne Frank's life is heartbreaking but inspiring. Her diary traces a life lived hidden from the Nazis, dominated by the fear of imminent discovery, but also by teenage obsessions and crushes.

Born in Frankfurt am Main in Germany, Anne's family fled to Amsterdam to escape the Third Reich's anti-Semitic policies. Anne was clever but impish, getting into trouble for chattering in school.

When Anne was eleven, the Nazis occupied Holland. As a Jewish family, the Franks were forced to submit to harsh rules: banned from owning a business, subject to curfews and made to wear yellow stars.

In June 1942, Anne's father Otto gave her a diary for her thirteenth birthday, in which she immediately started writing, detailing her everyday life. A month later, when her sister Margot received a notice to relocate to a work camp, the family went into hiding in an annexe above the offices of their old business, sharing the space with dentist Fritz Pfeffer and the van Pels family. Anne would go on to have a romantic relationship with sixteen-year-old Peter van Pels.

Throughout her family's incarceration in the annexe, Anne wrote in her diary about the tussles and arguments between house members, her frustrations, hopes and dreams, her terror at the war, her aspirations to be a journalist and her relationship with her sister.

In 1944, the Allies landed at Normandy and started to liberate Europe. Anne was ecstatic at the news, but, tragically, her family's hiding place was discovered two months later. Anne was sent to the Auschwitz-Birkenau concentration camp, where she had her head shaved and her arm tattooed, and was starved

In a film adaptation of her life, the starring role was offered to

AUDREY HEPBURN

and threatened with the gas chambers. She survived, only to be sent on to the Bergen-Belsen camp, where she died of typhus alongside her sister. Anne was just fifteen.

After the war, the only surviving member of the family, Otto, returned to Amsterdam. There he was given Anne's diary by his former secretary, Miep Gies, who had found it in the annexe. He edited it and it was published in 1947, followed by more editions around the world. Anne became a figurehead who humanised the nightmarish events of the Holocaust, and a role model for bravery and persistence in the face of oppression. She also resonated globally with teenagers frustrated with their families and lives.

Anne's father guarded her legacy with care and thought, using the profits from her diaries to keep the Anne Frank House museum open, to establish charitable foundations for education against racism, and to inform future generations about Nazism and persecution.

Another teenage girl whose diary has resonated with the world is Malala Yousafzai. Her (initially) anonymous blog detailed her defiant fight for her education against the Taliban. In January 2014, Malala, often referred to as the 'Anne Frank of Pakistan', was awarded the Anne Frank Award for moral courage.

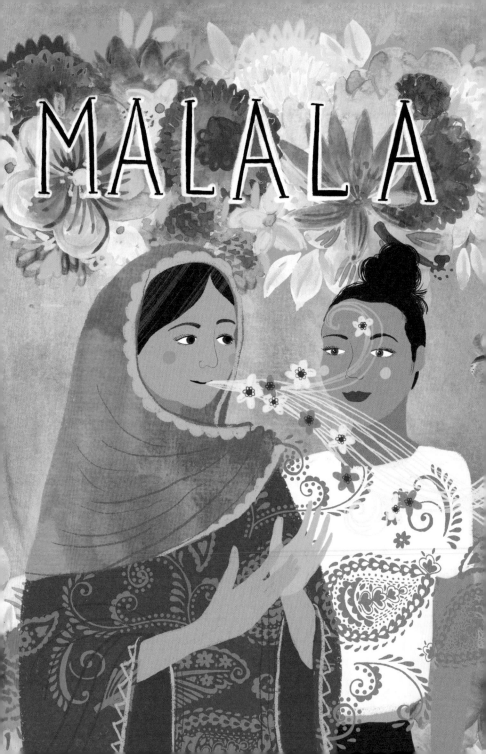

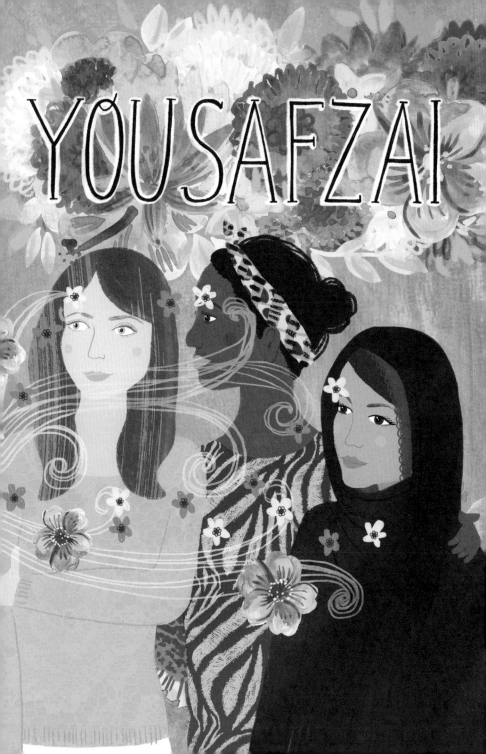

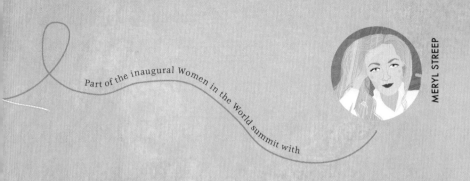

MERYL STREEP

DETERMINED TO get an education, regardless of the regime in charge of her country, Malala's story was brought to worldwide attention after she was shot in the head by militant Taliban forces. However, the shooting only served to strengthen her resolve to encourage girls around the world to attend school.

From the age of eleven, Malala published an anonymous online diary about life under Taliban rule in north-west Pakistan. She was passionate about her schooling, and demanded that girls should be educated. A year later, she started to appear in TV interviews, making her identity known to all. At fourteen, she was awarded the National Youth Peace Prize.

Malala's outspoken stance on girls' eduction made her an enemy of the Taliban and in 2012, when she was fifteen, a Taliban gunman boarded her school bus and shot her in the head in an attempted assassination. Amazingly, she survived. She was moved to the UK for treatment and recovery, after which she began attending school in Edgbaston. The attack resulted in a huge swell of support for Malala and, as well as continuing to attend school, she became an advocate for universal education, speaking around the world. On her sixteenth birthday, she addressed over 500 young education advocates at the United Nations. Her autobiography was an instant bestseller, and there has been a documentary made about her.

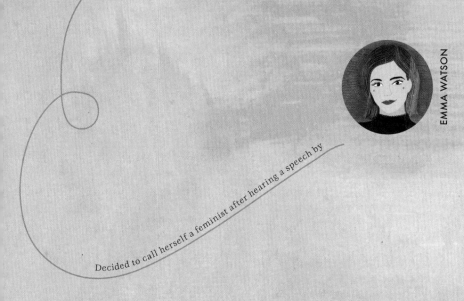

Decided to call herself a feminist after hearing a speech by

EMMA WATSON

In 2014, Malala became the youngest person to receive the Nobel Peace Prize. The then prime minister of Pakistan, Nawaz Sharif said, 'Her achievement is unparalleled and unequalled. Girls and boys of the world should take the lead from her struggle and commitment.'

On her eighteenth birthday, Malala opened a school in Lebanon for Syrian refugees, and demanded that world leaders stop spending on military budgets and start to fund education. In 2017, she became a United Nations Messenger of Peace, promoting girls' education. She travels the world, campaigning and calling for action.

In 2015, Malala teamed up with one of the most influential women in America, the then first lady, Michelle Obama, for the #62MillionGirls campaign, which aimed to get the millions of girls worldwide who were not currently receiving an education into schools. The pair launched the initiative at a music festival in New York, where both gave speeches. 'It is a book and a pen that can change the life of a child,' said Malala, 'It's not a gun.'

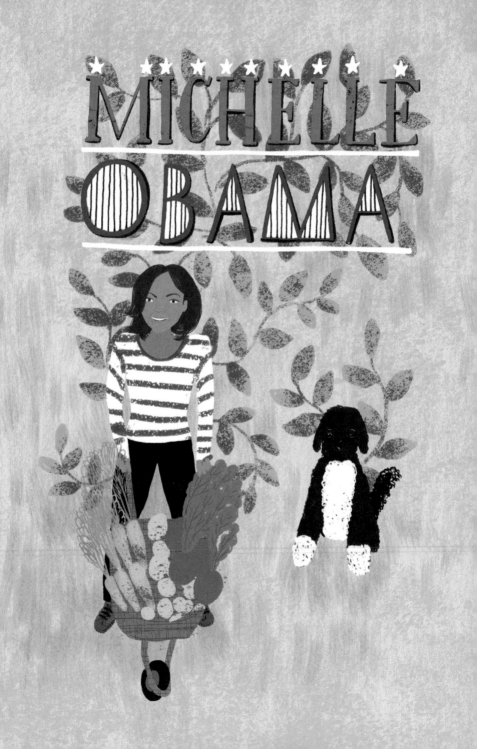

MICHELLE OBAMA

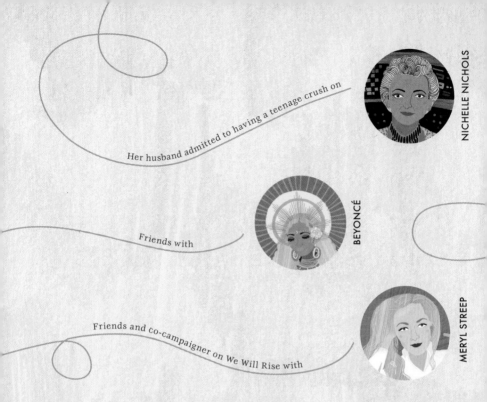

NICHELLE NICHOLS

Her husband admitted to having a teenage crush on

BEYONCÉ

Friends with

MERYL STREEP

Friends and co-campaigner on We Will Rise with

A LAWYER, writer and campaigner, Michelle Obama was catapulted into the public eye when her husband Barack became president of the USA. Her tenure in the White House showed her to be intelligent, wise and funny.

Michelle grew up in a modest bungalow in Chicago, Illinois. Money was tight – she and her brother slept in the living room – but the family was happy and close. Her parents put a strong emphasis on education, and Michelle went into her school's gifted programme. She graduated from Princeton University with a degree in sociology, before going on to Harvard to study law.

Michelle met Barack at Sidley Austin, a law firm where they both worked. The pair married in 1992 and went on to have two daughters, Malia and Sasha. Michelle started to work for the City of Chicago, then as the founding executive director of a leadership programme for young adults, after which she worked founding community service programmes at the University of Chicago.

Barack's political career started in 1996, when he was elected to the Illinois Senate, and gained real traction in 2005, when, as a rising star in the Democratic party, he was elected as a senator. When he decided to run for president in 2007, Michelle scaled down her professional life and campaigned alongside Barack, writing and making speeches, usually without notes. She also gained a reputation for telling wry, sarcastic stories about the Obamas' family life. Momentously, in 2009 Barack took office, and Michelle became the first lady.

Was written an open thank you note by

GLORIA STEINEM

Promoted her Let's Move campaign alongside

BILLIE JEAN KING

EMMA WATSON

asked her for a pep talk

Michelle used her position to support and inspire young people. One of her earliest moves was to establish a vegetable garden and beehives in the White House, which provided produce for the family's meals and vegetables to donate to food banks. She later wrote *American Grown* about her experiences, and built on the project to start the Let's Move! initiative, which worked to get young people active. Other campaigns included Joining Forces, which supported military families and veterans, and Reach Higher, which inspired young people to study at college. While she was in the White House, Michelle faced constant criticism on and offline from the press and the public about her appearance, policies and private life. She deflected them with humour and intelligence.

Her time as first lady was defined by her approachable persona, campaigning fire and obvious love for her children. However, despite her speech-giving skills and deep intelligence, she's ruled out running for the presidency.

Michelle Obama bade farewell to the White House in 2017, and her departure was marked by a *New York Times* feature called 'To the First Lady, With Love'. This consisted of thank-you letters from, among others, feminist Gloria Steinem, actress Rashida Jones, and novelist Chimamanda Ngozi Adichie, who decried the 'caricature' of the 'angry Black woman' that Michelle had been cast as.

THROUGH HER novels, essays and hugely influential public-speaking, writer Chimamanda has helped propel feminism into the mainstream.

Born in Enugu, in south-eastern Nigeria, Chimamanda's father was a professor of statistics at the University of Nigeria in Nsukka and her mother the university's first female registrar.

Chimamanda moved to the USA when she was nineteen, to study at Drexel University in Philadelphia, then transferred to Eastern Connecticut State University. After graduating, she studied creative writing at Johns Hopkins University, and went on to fellowships at Princeton and Harvard. Her first book, *Decisions*, a collection of poems, was published in 1997, followed by a play, *For Love of Biafra*, in 1998. Her big break came with her first novel, *Purple Hibiscus*, which was about a teenage Nigerian girl maturing and making sense of her dysfunctional family. The book was shortlisted for the 2004 Orange Prize for Fiction. Chimamanda's follow-up novel, *Half of a Yellow Sun*, was even more successful, and was made into a film in 2013.

However, it is Chimamanda's talks that have truly brought her into the spotlight. Her first TED talk in 2009, 'The Danger of a Single Story', explored how narratives can be misleading and the importance of multicultural representation. However, it was her second, 'We Should All Be Feminists', that broke the internet. It was an assured, impassioned definition of feminism for the twenty-first century. A print version of the speech made the bestseller lists, and the Swedish government distributed it to every sixteen-year-old in its country.

Chimamanda is married to Dr Ivara Esege, a professor of medicine. They have

CHIMAMANDA NGOZI ADICHIE

a baby, and live just outside Baltimore in Maryland, although she still has a house in Nigeria. With a career that feels as if it's far from peaking, watching Chimamanda soar higher will be fascinating.

Chimamanda's hugely popular 'We Should All Be Feminists' got even more attention when it was sampled by Beyoncé on her eponymous 2013 album, in the song 'Flawless'. Beyoncé's championing of feminism was welcomed by Chimamanda, who said it had brought her speech to a wider audience. She also criticised those who claimed Beyoncé wasn't a true believer, saying, 'Whoever says they're feminist is bloody feminist.'

One of *Time* magazine's Most Influential in 2015 alongside

EMMA WATSON

MISTY COPELAND

praised her for sampling *We Are All Feminists* on *Lemonade*

GLOBAL MEGASTAR and reigning voice of America, Beyoncé has used her fame as a musician and actress to incredible effect, maturing and emerging as an activist and philanthropist. She's been credited with helping to popularise feminism, particularly among young girls.

Born and raised in Houston, Texas, from the night a five-year-old Beyoncé saw Michael Jackson perform, she knew she wanted to do the same. By eight she was in an all-girl pop group, Girl's Tyme. Once she was into her teens, her father Mathew Knowles began managing the band. In 1997, the act solidified into Destiny's Child, a band with a shifting line-up, but most successfully featuring Beyoncé, Kelly Rowland and Michelle Williams. They went on to become one of the greatest musical trios of all time, with hits such as 'Bootylicious', 'Bills, Bills, Bills' and 'Survivor'. Beyoncé is credited as co-songwriter on most of their songs.

Beyoncé's first solo album, *Dangerously in Love*, was released in 2003, and went on to sell over 11 million copies worldwide. A confident, assured Beyoncé was clearly destined for a huge solo career, and Destiny's Child played their final shows in 2005. Beyoncé's performances were stellar – she could dance with precision and sass, perform technically brilliant and emotionally affecting vocals, and had an enormous, captivating stage presence. By 2006, she'd also started appearing in films, including *Dreamgirls*, where she played a Diana Ross-type character.

In 2008, Beyoncé married musician and businessman Jay-Z, whom she had first met when she was eighteen. The pair have gone on to have three children, although their relationship hasn't been without its issues — many of the lyrics in Beyoncé's 2016 album *Lemonade* made references to infidelities. How much they are a reflection of personal events, only Beyoncé and Jay-Z know.

Beyoncé has the knack of writing and performing songs that define their time: 'Crazy in Love', 'Single Ladies (Put a Ring on It)' and 'Run the World (Girls)' resonated further than dance floors, becoming their own cultural paradigms. Bey uses that universal appeal for good. After Hurricane Katrina she founded the Survivor Foundation for victims. She's also given thoughtful donations to substance-abuse charities and joined forces with her friend Michelle Obama to promote the first lady's healthy living initiatives. Beyoncé has also made political statements within her work, referencing the Black Panther party in her Super Bowl halftime show and speaking of her anger at police brutality and Donald Trump's withdrawal of protections for transgender students.

Always happy to share her influences, Beyoncé is a big admirer of 1920s dancer Josephine Baker – she pulled on a swinging banana skirt modelled on her heroine's at her 2006 Fashion Rocks performance. Her album *B'Day* was inspired in part by Josephine. Beyoncé said of her, 'It seemed like she just danced from her heart, and everything was so free.'

DARING BOTH on stage and off, Josephine Baker was a groundbreaking Jazz Age performer, who had a double life as a wartime spy.

Born to a drummer and an ex-music hall dancer in St Louis, Missouri, Josephine helped support her family from the age of eight. At eleven, she witnessed the St Louis race riots, which kickstarted her crusade against racism and discrimination. By fifteen, she'd run away, married and divorced.

Josephine had a talent for dancing — performing on street corners, then on tour in chorus lines. She visited Paris, falling in love with the tolerant city, and in 1925 opened in the sexy La Revue Nègre wearing only feathers. The following year, she performed at the Folies Bergère, sporting her famous skirt made of sixteen artificial bananas. Josephine subverted racial stereotypes, capitalising on Europe's fascination with the 'exotic' – she even appeared on stage with a pet cheetah. Her shows, films and records were hugely successful in France, but she failed to replicate those achievements in her more aggressively racist home nation. Eventually, she took French citizenship, and married industrialist Jean Lion.

During the Second World War, Josephine worked for the French Resistance. Her career meant she had access to high-level social events and travelled between countries. She smuggled messages in her underwear, wrote notes in invisible ink and gathered information. She was awarded medals and made a Chevalier of the Légion d'Honneur for her bravery.

JOSEPHINE

In her forties, Josephine started adopting children from different countries, and ended up living in a castle with twelve sons and daughters. She returned to the stage in 1949, in her imperial phase – bolstered by her medals and fired up about inequality. A tour in the USA was a huge success: she overturned racist club policies and was named the NAACP's Woman of the Year. She returned to the USA to speak at the 1963 March on Washington, drawing on her early experiences in Missouri.

By the late 1960s, Josephine's career was waning. Divorced and in debt, she was forced to give her beloved chateau over to creditors. She had one last hurrah — returning for a triumphant show in Paris, celebrating fifty years on stage. Four days later, she died in bed, surrounded by the glowing newspaper reviews.

Another woman who defied the fascists during the Second World War was thirteen-year-old Audrey Kathleen Ruston, a ballet fan who carried secret messages in her satin slippers, once helped to rescue an Allied pilot who was living rough, and who performed ballet recitals to raise money for the Dutch Resistance. Audrey went on to become the much-loved actress, Audrey Hepburn.

Appeared at the March on Washington, as did

MAHALIA JACKSON

BAKER

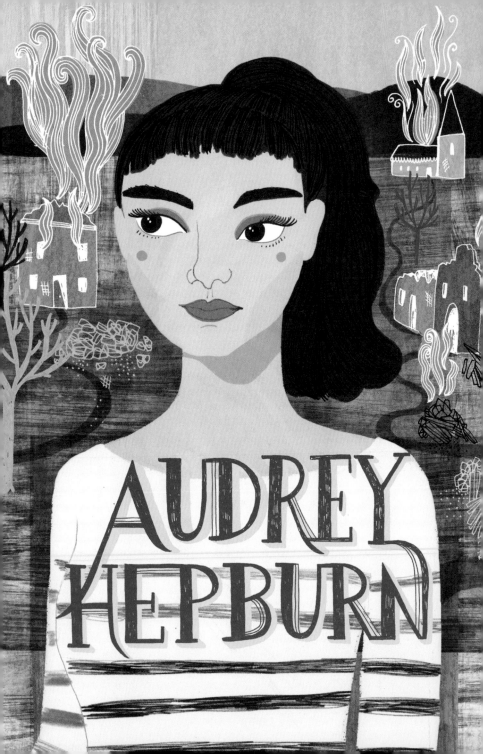

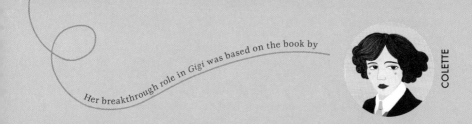

ELEGANT, TALENTED and charming, Audrey Hepburn's huge success as a movie star never dimmed her empathy.

Audrey was born in Belgium to a banker and a baroness, both of whom were fascists and split early in Audrey's life. Remarkably, the teenage Audrey rejected their beliefs, passing messages and raising money for the Dutch Resistance (she and her mother had moved to Holland at the start of the Second World War in the forlorn hope the neutral country would not be invaded by Germany). Like most of Holland at the time, Audrey was malnourished, which contributed towards her boyish frame and gamine looks. After the liberation, she attended ballet school in London and had a few minor speaking roles in films, but it was a Broadway production of *Gigi* that sparked her career. Hollywood came knocking, and two years later, her role as Princess Ann in *Roman Holiday* won her an Academy Award.

More stage and screen roles followed. During her stint on Broadway in *Ondine* she met her husband-to-be Mel Ferrer, going on to star alongside him on film in the more heavyweight *War and Peace*. The couple would have one son: Sean.

Another hugely important relationship for Audrey was with clothing designer Hubert de Givenchy, who she persuaded to provide the costumes for the romantic comedy *Sabrina*. Givenchy went on to collaborate with Audrey on the outfits for all of her contemporarily set films.

Audrey's expressive face, comedy chops and graceful physicality made her a star. She danced gaily through *Funny Face*, won a third Academy Award nomination for her thoughtful performance in *The Nun's Story*, played the 'jazziest role of her career' as Holly Golightly in *Breakfast at Tiffany's*, and shone in the extraordinarily popular *My Fair Lady*. She gained her final Academy Award nomination for the intense thriller *Wait Until Dark*, produced by her soon-to-be ex-husband. Audrey married psychiatrist Andrea Dotti in 1969, and the pair had a son, Luca, in 1970.

Going into semi-retirement from 1967, Audrey chose to devote time to her family. She became a goodwill ambassador for UNICEF in 1989. In that role she travelled to, among other places, Ethiopia to help with the famine work, Turkey to immunise children, Sudan to raise awareness of the effects of civil war, and to Somalia, where the starvation was 'apocalyptic'. Audrey was shaken, perhaps vividly reminded of her early years. She was awarded the Presidential Medal of Freedom, and after her death in 1993 she won a posthumous Academy Award for her humanitarian work.

One of Audrey's most famous and loved performances was as the infamous Holly Golightly in *Breakfast at Tiffany's*. The film was an adaptation of a book by Truman Capote, who is thought to have based the impish character of Holly on his friend and co-worker at *Harper's Bazaar* and the *New Yorker*, writer Maeve Brennan.

MAEVE BRENNAN'S pen portraits of her beloved adopted home of New York sang from the page, but her descent into mental illness and alcoholism meant that she never built on her early work.

Born in Dublin, the 1916 Easter Rising provided the prelude to Maeve's birth. Her parents were Republicans, actively involved in the armed insurrection, but when Maeve was seventeen the Brennans moved to America – her father had been appointed the first Irish ambassador to the country. Graduating from Washington's American University with a degree in English, Maeve was drawn to Greenwich Village, New York, home to free-thinkers, drinkers and bohemians.

Tiny, always impeccably groomed, in her large dark glasses and black clothes and with her chestnut hair swept upwards, Maeve wore Chanel's Cuir de Russie, the scent designed for women who dared to smoke. She wrote for fashion magazine *Harper's Bazaar*, then when she was thirty-two was offered a staff job at the *New Yorker*.

Maeve's column, written under the pseudonym 'The Long-Winded Lady', described the city with a melancholic, sharp, detached eye, revelling in poignant moments. She also wrote short stories set in Dublin, which would later be the bedrock for the revival of interest in her work.

An eccentric with a sharp wit, Maeve swore, drank and lived in transient fashion. But the barfly lifestyle came at a cost. A marriage of five years to the *New Yorker*'s equally sybaritic managing editor was a disaster. Maeve's mental health

was fragile, and by the late 1960s, when the first collections of her work were published, her behaviour had become erratic. By the 1970s, she was plagued by alcoholism, with no regular place to sleep – spending periods in hospital, or silently sitting outside the *New Yorker* offices. In the 1980s, she vanished, finally traced by a fan after over a decade, in 1992, to a nursing home. She died a year later. Her books are now back in print and she's appreciated as a skilled short-story writer.

The *New Yorker* had been set up in 1925, with Dorothy Parker as part of its editorial board. Equally sharp-witted, and happiest with a cigarette and drink in hand, Dorothy predated Maeve at the publication by sixteen years, but her life's trajectory followed the same path of turbulence and reclusiveness.

The *New Yorker* also published the fiction of

VIRGINIA WOOLF

WHILE DOROTHY Parker was at the epicentre of the ultimate in-crowd – the Algonquin Round Table – and her 'flapper verse' painted dazzling pictures of Jazz Age New York, her obsession with suicide and self-destructive tendencies were never far from the surface.

Dorothy's mother died when she was five, leaving her at the mercy of her despised father and stepmother, who she referred to, acidly, as 'the housekeeper'. Her father died penniless, so Dorothy worked — first as a piano player, then as a caption writer at *Vogue*. Her precise style quickly landed her a job at *Vanity Fair*, where she became the publication's drama critic. She fell into the habit of spending every lunchtime at the Algonquin Hotel with fellow writers Robert Benchley and Robert E. Sherwood. The trio expanded into a cast of dozens, known as the Round Table, whose sardonic wit was eagerly reported in newspaper columns. However, Dorothy's acerbic commentary proved too much for *Vanity Fair*, and she was fired in 1920.

Dorothy's love life was scrappy. She married Edwin Pond Parker II, a morphine and alcohol addict, in 1917, but divorced in 1928 after she had a number of affairs. She later married actor Alan Campbell – twice, neither time successfully.

In 1925, Dorothy helped establish the *New Yorker* magazine, which published many of her poems. She also wrote plays, short stories and, after a move to Hollywood, film scripts. Her film-writing career blossomed to begin with, but faltered in the late 1940s, after she was accused of being a communist.

Dorothy *had* been an activist – she supported the civil rights movement and Spanish Civil War loyalists, and was arrested when she protested against the executions of a pair of anarchists. On her death — which came after a long period of being closeted away with only lonely morning cocktails and her dog for company — she left all her money, copyrights and royalties to Martin Luther King Jr, whom she had never met, but admired greatly.

Martin Luther King Jr also played a major role in the life of Nichelle Nichols. The actor was thinking of leaving *Star Trek* after the first series when she met Dr King at a fundraising dinner for the NAACP. He convinced her that, as one of the only Black characters on TV in a leading part, and a vital role model, she should stay.

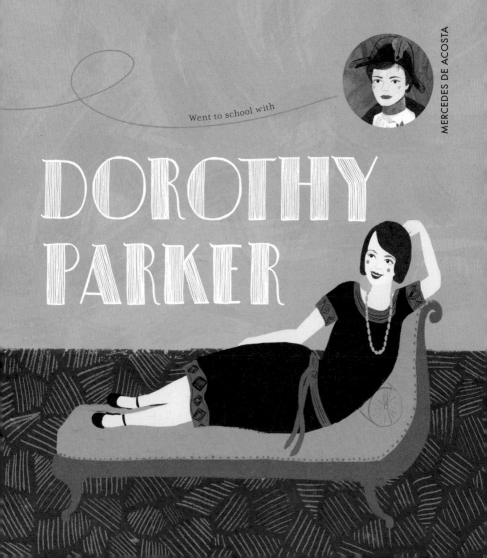

MERCEDES DE ACOSTA

Went to school with

DOROTHY PARKER

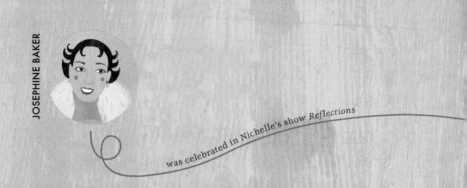

was celebrated in Nichelle's show Reflections

NICHELLE BOLDLY went where no African American woman had gone before – playing a character on a TV show who wasn't subservient.

Nichelle was born Grace Nichols, and grew up in the very small town of Robbins, Illinois, where her father Samuel was the mayor and magistrate. The family moved to Chicago, where Nichelle studied at the Chicago Ballet Academy. She started her career as a singer and dancer: performing with the Duke Ellington and Lionel Hampton Orchestras, appearing alongside Sammy Davis Jr in the film version of *Porgy and Bess*, and taking on heavyweight stage roles, for which she was nominated twice for a Sarah Siddons Award.

Nichelle's big break came after an appearance on *The Lieutenant*, a TV series about racial prejudice, which was produced by Gene Roddenberry. Two years later, Roddenberry offered her a major role in his new science-fiction series, *Star Trek*. Nichelle's role was that of Lieutenant Uhura, the name a twist on *uhuru* – Swahili for freedom. Purely by playing an assured, intelligent woman on equal footing with the rest of the cast, Nichelle broke boundaries, but the show busted more taboos in 1968 when Uhura kissed the white Captain Kirk. It is widely regarded as the first interracial kiss on network US television.

Nichelle's interest in space exploration extended beyond her acting role. After the cancellation of *Star Trek*, she went on to work for NASA in a very successful drive to recruit more minority and female workers. In 2015, she even got to fly aboard NASA's Stratospheric Observatory in a high-altitude flight.

Nichelle continued to have a healthy acting and singing career, but was always proud to revisit Uhura – she appeared in the *Star Trek* movies, released a *Star Trek*-themed album, and remained a star attraction at Trekker conventions.

Nichelle was an inspiration to many: Whoopi Goldberg has cited her as an influence and President Obama told her that as a teen he had a crush on her. Astronaut Mae Jemison is candid about Nichelle being a role model. She said, 'She used her celebrity to bring in applications – and she did it on her own.' After Mae achieved her dream of space travel, she met Nichelle at a *Star Trek* convention in Florida, and went on to appear in an episode of *Star Trek: The Next Generation*.

NICHELLE NICHOLS

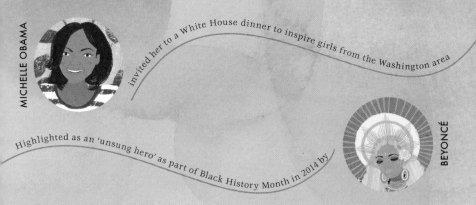

MAE JEMISON was not only the first African American woman in space, but a doctor, Peace Corps volunteer, teacher and businesswoman.

Brought up in Chicago, Illinois, Mae wanted to be a scientist from an early age, and her parents supported her wholeheartedly. She was a clever student, inspired by the world around her and by current affairs. She was fascinated by 1969's Apollo moon landing, but irritated that there were no female astronauts.

Alongside her academic studies, Mae learned to dance, and considered a stage career. However, she chose medical school over professional dancing, and got a scholarship to Stanford University when she was only sixteen. As well as heading the Black Student Union, she gained degrees in chemical engineering and African and African American studies, then went on to study for a doctorate of medicine at Cornell University.

Mae used her education for good, joining the Peace Corps in 1983 and serving in Liberia and Sierra Leone, where she supervised the care of volunteers and worked on vaccine research. On her return to the USA, she worked as a doctor, but cleaved to her childhood dream of becoming an astronaut. Motivated by seeing Sally Ride become the first American woman in space, Mae applied to join NASA, and was accepted into the astronaut programme in 1987.

It wasn't until 1992 that she went on her first and only space flight, as a mission specialist on a cooperative flight between the USA and Japan. Alongside six other astronauts, Mae made 127 orbits around the earth onboard the shuttle Endeavour. She conducted bone-cell research and motion-sickness experiments, and returned home after almost 200 hours in space. Staying true to her Trekker past, every morning she greeted her base with one of the show's catchphrases: 'Hailing frequencies open.'

Mae went on to teach at Dartmouth College and Cornell, where she campaigned to encourage minority students' interest in science. She's also founded two tech-based companies and is a passionate public speaker.

Mae took a few carefully chosen objects into space with her. As well as African art pieces to represent her heritage, she also took a photo of Bessie Coleman, the pioneering African American pilot. She later described how she hadn't heard about Bessie until after she entered the NASA programme and felt cheated, calling her audacious and daring — 'all those things that our children aspire to'.

BEYONCÉ

BESSIE 'QUEEN Bess' Coleman soared high above racism, gender discrimination and poverty to become the first American to gain an international pilot's licence and the first African American and Native American woman to hold a US pilot's licence.

Bessie was born into poverty and oppression. Her parents were Texas sharecroppers: her mother African American and her father (who left the family when Bessie was young) Cherokee and African American. She grew up in a world where the wrath of the KKK was real, and cotton-picking work was harsh and paid little. As well as studying hard Bessie helped to provide for her twelve brothers and sisters. After graduating she travelled to Oklahoma to attend college, but she couldn't afford to support herself so returned home.

Undaunted in her desire to escape, at twenty-three Bessie moved to Chicago, Illinois, where she worked as a manicurist in barber's shops. She'd spend time in the shops chatting to pilots who'd returned from the First World War, which sparked her interest in flight. She worked and saved, and got financial backing from African American community leaders. Then in 1920, she travelled to Paris to learn to fly.

Within six months, Bessie had a licence and was itching to get off the ground. However, in order to make money and achieve her dream of opening her own flying school for African Americans, she realised that she would have to become a stunt flyer.

On her return to the USA, Bessie was a sensation – unafraid and with plenty of pizzazz, she'd whirl and twirl in graceful loops and figures of eight above adoring crowds, and didn't let accidents deter her. When a parachutist once failed to turn up for a show, Bessie slung one on and jumped out of a plane herself.

She was offered a role in a film, *Shadow and Sunshine*. However, it became apparent that her role would involve her wearing tattered clothes and playing to a stereotype, so she refused to proceed. Bessie would make more principled stands: she refused to perform at airshows that denied admission to Black people, and she spoke and lectured, encouraging more African American women to fly.

Tragically, in 1926, after purchasing a badly maintained plane that veered out of control and crashed, Bessie and her mechanic died. Five thousand people in Orlando, Florida and 15,000 in Chicago paid their respects to Bessie at memorial services. In Chicago, mourners sang 'Jesus, Savior, Pilot Me'. This hymn would go on to be interpreted to incredible effect by a woman who moved to Chicago the year after Bessie died: Mahalia Jackson. Both women lived in the area of Chicago named Bronzeville, and Bessie had been a member of the congregation of the Pilgrim Baptist Church – the place Mahalia would go on to help become the 'birthplace of gospel'.

MAHALIA JACKSON'S deep contralto voice soundtracked the struggle of African Americans towards equality. She became an international star, and used her fame and majestic presence to great effect on civil rights marches.

Mahalia's New Orleans childhood in Louisiana was filled with the sound of music: gospel drifted from church doors, jazz bands played on street corners, and Mahalia basked in the influence of blues artists such as Bessie Smith and Ma Rainey. She lived in a tiny house with twelve other people, which was ruled by the iron fist of her aunt Mahala. Church became Mahalia's second home, and her impressive voice rang to the rafters of the Mount Moriah Baptist Church.

At the age of sixteen, Mahalia joined the great migration to Chicago, Illinois in search of employment. She scratched around for domestic work, but found more fulfilment touring professionally in gospel choirs.

Mahalia was determined that she would never sing secular tunes, a promise she kept in her professional life that lost her a contract with Decca and her marriage. But her professional partnership with composer Thomas A. Dorsey birthed the 'Golden Age of Gospel'.

Her breakthrough came with the single 'Move On Up a Little Higher', which sold 8 million copies and made her a star in the US and Europe. Mahalia became known as the 'world's greatest

gospel singer' and headlined venues such as Carnegie Hall, where she played to an integrated audience. She made cameo appearances in films, played the Newport Jazz Festival with Duke Ellington and sang at John F. Kennedy's inaugural ball. Perhaps the pinnacle of her career was her performance at 1963's March on Washington, where her friend Martin Luther King Jr made his famous address. Some witnesses claim that Mahalia called to him during the speech — 'Tell them about your dream, Martin' – spurring him into his legendary climax.

Mahalia died at the age of sixty, and there were two memorial services for her: one in Chicago, where 50,000 people filed past her coffin and 6,000 people attended the commemoration, and one in New Orleans, attended by thousands more.

Alongside Mahalia in the NAACP, and a fellow friend of Martin Luther King Jr, was the more overtly political Nina Simone.

Whilst on final tour she met

INDIRA GANDHI

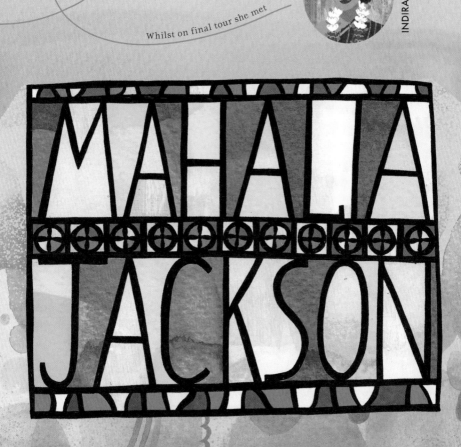

MAHALIA JACKSON

RAGING, RIGHTEOUS and with incandescent talent, Nina Simone ripped up genre boundaries and lived an uncompromising life.

Born Eunice Kathleen Waymon in North Carolina, Nina's prodigious concert piano-playing talent shone early. Funded by local supporters, she attended the Juilliard School in New York, then applied for a scholarship at the Curtis Institute of Music in Philadelphia. Despite a stunning audition, she was rejected — because, she believed, of her race. The experience helped fuel an anger that propelled her through her career.

In 1958, Nina had a brief marriage to beatnik Don Ross, and recorded her breakthrough single, 'I Loves You, Porgy'. Her follow-up album, *Little Girl Blue*, was a success, and she went on to record dozens more.

By 1961, Nina was married to Andrew Stroud and in 1962 she had given birth to a child, Lisa. Nina's relationship with Stroud, who was to become her manager, was turbulent and abusive. In addition, Nina, later diagnosed as bipolar, found her temper difficult to control; she would lash out physically and admonished misbehaving audience members.

By the mid-1960s, Nina's music had become associated with the civil rights movement. Her friend, the playwright Lorraine Hansberry, encouraged her to funnel her anger into her art. Nina later wrote: 'We never talked about men or clothes. It was always Marx, Lenin and revolution — real girls' talk.' She played a set that included her protest anthem 'Mississippi Goddam' at the end of a Selma to Montgomery civil rights march in 1965, where she met Martin Luther King Jr.

However, Nina was convinced that her politics crippled her career. Disillusioned, she left the USA in the 1970s, ending up living in countries including Barbados, Liberia and Switzerland, before settling in France in the 1990s.

During the 1980s, a new generation discovered Nina through CD rereleases and her music being used on adverts. In 2003, two days before her death, the Curtis Institute awarded her an honorary degree, and she passed away in the knowledge that her colossal talent had been recognised, both critically and commercially.

Nina was friends with fellow political activist Angela Davis. Angela was an admirer of Nina's work and recognised that Nina's performances at protests were often the sole female contribution. When Angela was in jail, Nina visited, arriving late. The delay was due to her bringing Angela a red, helium-filled balloon that she'd had to argue through security. Angela kept it as a treasure even after it deflated.

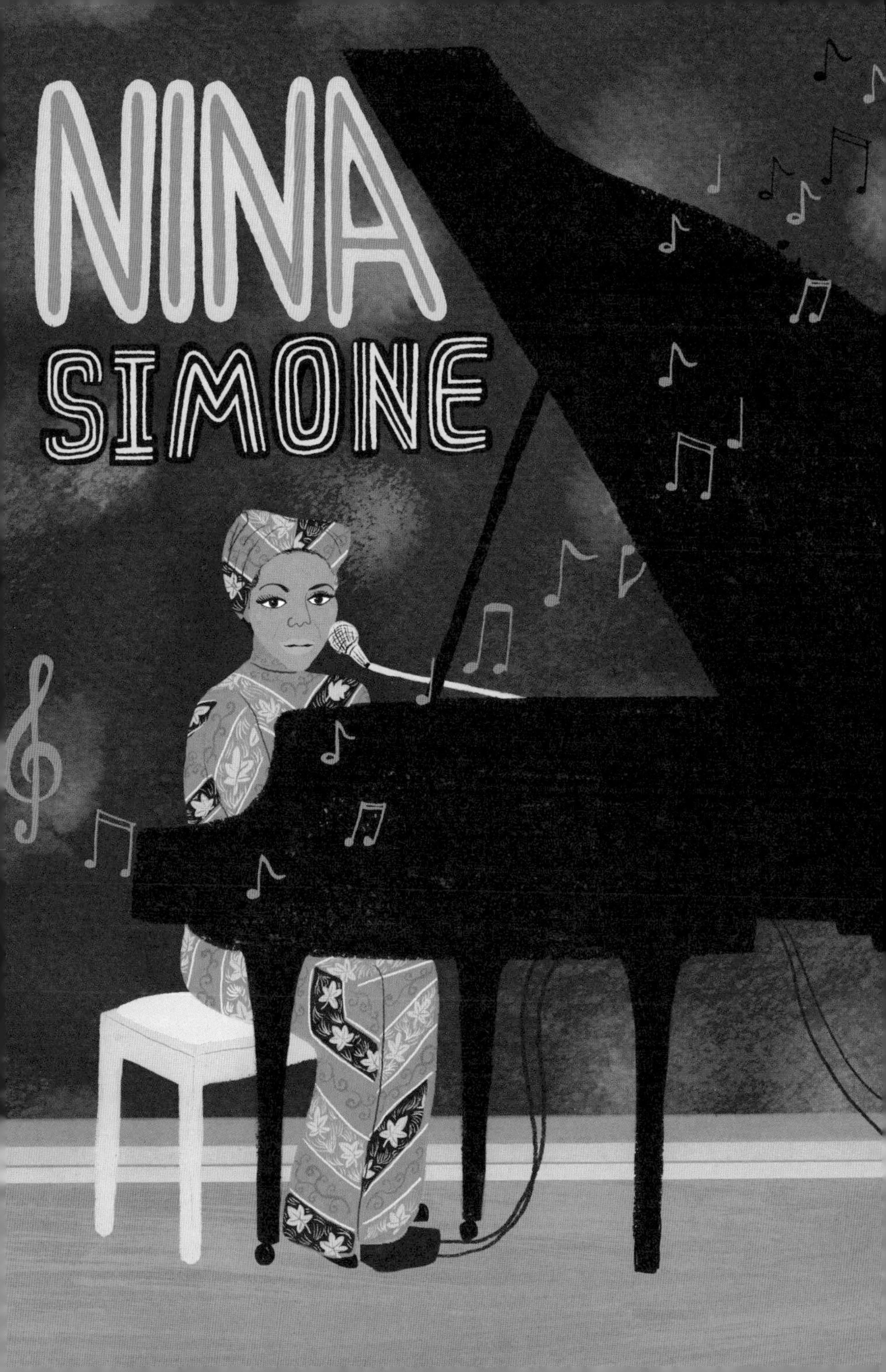
NINA
SIMONE

Was imprisoned for her political activism, as was

SYLVIA PANKHURST

FIGHTING FOR racial equality, Angela Davis pushed for women's issues within the civil rights movement, as well as challenging the capitalist establishment in the USA.

Born in Birmingham, Alabama, a place that was to be at the centre of the action for civil rights, Angela Yvonne Davis spent her childhood in church and at the Girl Scouts, with whom she marched to protest racial segregation. During her teenage years, Angela's mother, Sallye Bell Davis, became national officer of the Southern Negro Youth Congress, and Angela's day-to-day life became one of communist politics and activism — as a teen, she organised interracial study groups that were broken up by the police. At fifteen, she moved to New York for her high school education, where she met more radical thinkers and joined a communist youth group.

After gaining her undergraduate degree in philosophy from Brandeis University in Massachusetts, Angela spent two years in Germany, then returned to the University of California. There she joined the Black Panthers, and was active within all-Black communist group the Che-Lumumba Club.

Angela took up a professorship in philosophy at the university, then made a trip to Cuba, which reinforced her beliefs that a socialist system would provide a bedrock for racial equality. On her return, she discovered that the university board, encouraged by California governor Ronald Reagan, was trying to fire her. After a legal battle, she got her job back, but was released again by the board a year later.

After a violent protest at a courthouse, where four people were killed, Angela was charged with kidnapping, conspiracy and murder. She fled the west coast, but was arrested in New York and sent back to California on remand. An enormous, international 'Free Angela Davis' campaign, supported by the likes of the Rolling Stones, Bob Dylan and Yoko Ono, all of whom wrote songs dedicated to Angela, prefaced her acquittal in 1972 after sixteen months' imprisonment.

She became an in-demand lecturer around the world, and resumed her teaching career in 1980 at San Francisco State University. That year, Angela also married photographer Hilton Braithwaite, but divorced three years later. She came out as a lesbian in 1997.

Angela continues to be a fervent political activist, focusing on prison reform, racism, sexism and American imperialism.

Marching for women's rights in big sunglasses, high boots and miniskirts alongside Angela Davis was Gloria Steinem. Gloria was the chair of the fundraising committee of the Free Angela Davis campaign, and continues to be a close ally of Angela to this day.

was the inspiration for the original title of *Ms.* magazine

EVER CALL yourself 'Ms'? You've got journalist and pioneering second-wave feminist Gloria Steinem to thank for popularising the term.

Gloria's grandmother was a suffragette, educational campaigner and Holocaust heroine, and Gloria inherited her forebear's fire and drive. Gloria's childhood was itinerant — each year her family would travel, buying and selling antiques, from Michigan to Florida and back, until her father left the family. Her mother's mental health was fragile, and she had trouble keeping down a job, so Gloria cared for her.

Gloria graduated from college in 1956, spent time studying in India, then embarked on a career as a journalist. Women's issues were a regular topic for her, but she became an 'active feminist' when she covered a meeting about abortion for New York magazine. She went on to write articles such as 'After Black Power, Women's Liberation' for the publication.

In 1971, Gloria joined with 300 women to form the National Women's Political Caucus, aiming to get more women into political life. Shortly afterwards, in 1972, she co-founded *Ms.*, a feminist magazine that tackled issues such as domestic violence, pornography, same-sex marriage and female genital mutilation – many of which were being addressed for the first time in public. The cover of the first full-length issue featured an (unpaid) housewife-goddess in the style of Vishnu. It sold out its 300,00 print run within eight days.

Parallel to her journalistic career, Gloria was active in campaigning, becoming a figurehead for second-wave feminists, and was involved in Democratic party politics.

Her diagnosis with breast cancer in 1986 didn't stop her momentum; with treatment, Gloria beat the disease, resumed campaigning, and in 1992 set up Choice USA (now called URGE), a pro-choice organisation focused on younger people.

Perhaps the biggest surprise Gloria sprung on the world was her marriage at the age of sixty-six to animal-rights activist David Bale. Tragically, he died three years later of brain lymphoma. Gloria's work continued. She hosted a TV show, *Woman*, and continued to write books and campaign. She says, 'The idea of retiring is as foreign to me as the idea of hunting.'

While Gloria was fighting sexism on the streets, a young tennis player, Billie Jean King, was leading an equally passionate battle against chauvinism on the courts. The two were friends and allies; Billie Jean was on the list of women who admitted to having abortions published in the first issue of *Ms.* magazine. Gloria also helped Billie Jean to found *womenSports* magazine and the Women's Sports Foundation, which helped women athletes obtain college scholarships.

Was inspired by the leadership qualities of

NOT ONLY was Billie Jean King one of the greatest tennis players of all time, she also served smash after smash to inequality both on and off the court.

The daughter of working-class, Methodist parents, who supported and encouraged her love of sport, Billie Jean started to play tennis at the age of eleven, progressing quickly to play in tournaments. At fifteen, Billie Jean's hard-hitting style brought her to the attention of ex-Grand Slam winner Alice Marble, with whom she began to train.

When Billie Jean was seventeen, despite being unseeded, she and Karen Hantze won the Wimbledon women's doubles title. Supporting herself by teaching tennis, Billie Jean battled through tournaments, eventually winning her first major singles championship at Wimbledon in 1966. She would go on to win thirty-nine Grand Slam titles in total, peaking in 1972, when she won three.

In 1970, Billie Jean joined the inaugural Virginia Slims Circuit for women and started to earn large sums of money, but was frustrated that she and her fellow players earned less than men. She used that fury to positive effect, supporting the Title IX law, which gave women protection against discrimination and enabled them to take up college scholarships – something she had been denied.

In 1973, threatening a boycott of the US Open worked wonders: it became the first major tournament to offer men and women the same prize amount. Buoyed, the following year, Billie Jean and her then husband Larry King set up the mixed-gender World Team Tennis league.

Her activism did not go unnoticed. One of tennis' most chauvinistic players was former Wimbledon winner Bobby Riggs. Bobby had an eye for a hustle, challenging female players to beat him. Billie Jean took him on in September 1973 in the televised 'Battle of the Sexes' match and won in straight sets, a potent symbol to over 50 million viewers of the emerging women's movement worldwide.

Retiring in 1975, there were more battles to be fought for Billie Jean. Following a 'palimony' lawsuit brought by her ex-lover Marilyn Barnett – which forced her out of the closet and made her the first prominent female athlete to come out as a lesbian – Billie Jean lost all her endorsements. However, she became a figurehead for the LGBT community, and has won the Presidential Medal of Freedom for her work in the area.

A contemporary of Billie Jean King, Oprah Winfrey has also won the Presidential Medal of Freedom, and is equally passionate about parity of pay for women. Billie Jean featured in the 'Women Who Changed the World' episode of Oprah's self-titled show, alongside Gloria Steinem. Both Billie Jean and Oprah took centre stage at the White House Council on Women and Girls' United State of Women summit in 2016.

Has interviewed and is good friends with

BEYONCÉ

Friends with and recipient of an award named after

BILLIE JEAN KING

Has interviewed and admires

MERYL STREEP

CARVING OUT her own American dream, Oprah packs more into a week than most of us do in a lifetime. She's a talk-show host, an actor, runs a TV network and has her own magazine. She's the richest African American person, an activist and philanthropist. All this, and she's also credited with singlehandedly re-sparking America's interest in reading through her pioneering book club.

Oprah's childhood was tough. She was born to a teenage single mother in rural Mississippi, lived a life in poverty – she used to wear dresses made of potato sacks – and was shunted between relatives, until, at thirteen, she ran away from home. She fell pregnant at fourteen, but sadly her son died in early infancy, and she was sent to live with her father. He focused on her education, and Oprah began to shine, being voted most popular girl at high school and winning an oratory scholarship to Tennessee State

University. While she was at university, Oprah worked part-time reading the news at a local radio station and won the Miss Black Tennessee beauty pageant.

Oprah's stellar career started in television: she worked as a news anchor in Nashville and Baltimore, Maryland before moving to Illinois to host ailing talk show *AM Chicago*. Within months, the sympathetic, funny, confident Oprah had turned around the ratings. The programme was renamed *The Oprah Winfrey Show*, and two years later began broadcasting nationally. Initially, it was admirably bold but focused on dysfunction. Oprah drew empathetically on her own turbulent life – her weight-loss battles, her love affairs and her sexual abuse during childhood – and her guests trusted, liked and opened up to her.

However, in the mid-1990s, Oprah's attitudes started to mature, and she rebranded the programme to become

Has championed and supported

has been interviewed by and commissioned to write an article for her

is a long-time collaborator

more positive, covering social issues and inspirational stories. In 1996, she added the popular Oprah's Book Club segment, which made an overnight bestseller of every book featured. The show came to an end in 2011.

Parallel to her TV career, Oprah had careers in acting – she received an Academy Award nomination for her role in *The Color Purple*, writing (she's co-authored five books) and media – she gained ownership of *The Oprah Winfrey Show* in 1986, established a new radio channel, co-founded women's cable television network Oxygen, and runs TV channel OWN: Oprah Winfrey Network. Her magazine, *O, The Oprah Magazine*, was named as the most successful magazine start-up of all time.

As one of the highest-paid entertainers in the world, and one of the wealthiest women in America, Oprah puts her money to good use, making contributions

to, among others, the Harold Washington Library and her alma mater.

Oprah has interviewed a huge number of major celebrities, including a twelve-year-old Emma Watson, with whom she spoke on the release of the second *Harry Potter* movie. The pair have much in common: both are keen practitioners of mindfulness and both have set up successful book clubs. In February 2016, Emma recommended her second book, *The Color Purple* by Alice Walker, saying, 'A film was made of the book in 1985 by Steven Spielberg. It was Oprah Winfrey's film debut and introduced Whoopi Goldberg (I love both of these women).'

BELOVED BY millions for her portrayal of Hermione Granger in the *Harry Potter* films, Emma Watson has transcended her child-star status. She is now an acclaimed actress, dedicated student, and women's rights activist, unafraid to fight online trolls as well as those found in the corridors of Hogwarts.

Born in Paris, Emma, her mother and brother moved to England following her parents' divorce. She was ten when she landed the role of Hermione, a moment that was to cast a transformative spell on her life. Her performance was critically acclaimed and the film hugely successful. Emma was instantly, ragingly, popular with Muggles worldwide, and she went on to star in a further seven of the franchise's films. Her career continued to fly after the series, with roles in more mature films

such as *The Perks of Being a Wallflower* and *My Week with Marilyn*.

Emma studied hard with her tutors on set, achieving high grades, and went on to attend Oxford and Brown universities, graduating from the latter in 2014 with a degree in English Literature. Parallel to her film career and studies, Emma worked in fashion: modelling for Burberry and Lancôme, appearing on countless magazine covers and endorsing a collection for fair-trade clothing label People Tree. While working with People Tree in 2010, Emma visited the workers in the slums of Bangladesh, where her interest in the rights of all girls to education was solidified. She pledged her support to Camfed, an organisation that supports girls education in sub-Saharan Africa.

In 2014, Emma was made a UN Women Goodwill Ambassador, and in 2014 she launched her HeForShe campaign with a speech at their headquarters. Malala Yousafzai later told Emma that she started labelling herself a feminist due to Emma's speech. The campaign was high impact and Emma had to ride out rough treatment on social media, including a threat to publish nude photos online, but she attracted huge amounts of positive attention too. The following year, Emma appeared in *Time* magazine's '100 Most Influential' list, her brand of feminism being praised as gutsy and smart. On the cover of that issue of *Time*, and alongside Emma in the 100 influencers, was ballet dancer Misty Copeland, described by her hero, gymnast Nadia Comăneci, as 'a model for all young girls'.

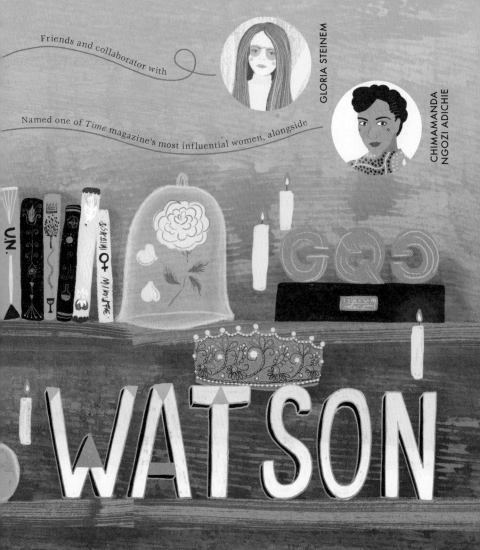

Friends and collaborator with

GLORIA STEINEM

Named one of *Time* magazine's most influential women, alongside

CHIMAMANDA NGOZI ADICHIE

WATSON

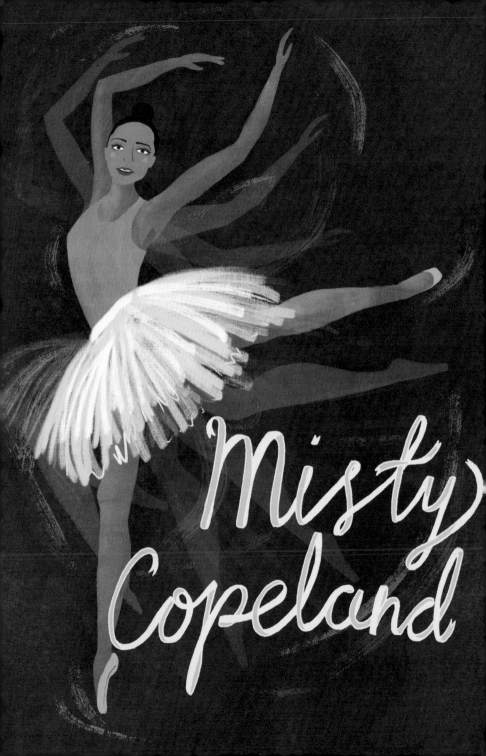

Misty Copeland

CHIMAMANDA
NGOZI ADICHIE

THE FIRST African American dancer to be appointed principal at the American Ballet Theatre, Misty Copeland has redefined the storyline, skin colour and even the body shape of the traditional ballerina.

Misty's family background was chaotic: her mother had a series of marriages and relationships, and Misty lived with her five brothers and sisters. However, she escaped the tumultuousness at school, where she was on the drill team. Spotting the thirteen-year-old Misty's talent, her teacher encouraged her into ballet classes, where Cynthia Bradley (a teacher at a small local ballet school) gave her free lessons and equipment.

Cynthia was adamant that Misty's prodigious abilities should be nurtured. Misty's family was now in a twin-suite motel room, so Cynthia took her into her home. Home-schooled from the age of fifteen to allow more time to dance, Misty started to win competitions and awards, and attended prestigious workshops. Her nascent career lost its perfect balance when her mother, resenting the Bradleys' 'snobbishness', embarked on a custody battle for Misty. This compelled her to rejoin her family, return to school and train only in the afternoon.

At seventeen, Misty joined the American Ballet Theatre training programme in New York, going on to their studio company, then progressing to the corps de ballet, where she was the only Black female dancer among eighty. Misty has been vocal about her struggles with eating disorders at this time, feeling under pressure to conform to the 'ideal' ballerina shape. She says that as she gained confidence as a performer and with herself, she began to embrace her muscles and curves.

Misty's roles became more prominent, and she was noted as a stand-out dancer. In 2007, at twenty-four, she became one of the youngest ABT solo dancers, her sophistication shining through in productions such as *The Nutcracker, Bach Partita* and *The Firebird*. Misty says that it was 'overwhelming' to see audiences for *The Firebird* that were 50 per cent African American. Outside of the rarefied world of ballet, in 2009 Misty was cast in Prince's 'Crimson and Clover' video, as well as dancing for him on tour.

Misty's greatest achievement was yet to come. In 2015, she was appointed principal ballerina at ABT – the first in the company's seventy-five-year history, and one of fewer than ten African American principal ballerinas in America's history. In 2016, she starred in a production of *Romeo and Juliet* at the Metropolitan Opera House. However, for one night in the show's run, the role was turned over to another remarkable dancer, for whom the part had become totemic: the fifty-three-year-old Alessandra Ferri.

PIROUETTING FROM being one of the youngest ever prima ballerinas in the UK's Royal Ballet to performing as one of the oldest, Alessandra oh-so-elegantly broke the dance world's conventions and boundaries.

Born in Milan, Alessandra studied at La Scala Ballet School, then the Royal Ballet School, after which, at fifteen, she joined the Royal Ballet. There she became the muse of choreographer Sir Kenneth MacMillan, being made a principal at nineteen. Her first major role was as the darkly passionate Mary Vetsera in *Mayerling*, followed by a fierce Juliet in *Romeo and Juliet*. Many thought she'd go on to lead the company, but in an unexpected move, at the request of Mikhail Baryshnikov, she relocated to the American Ballet Theatre. There she enjoyed tougher training and great critical acclaim in the title roles of Giselle, Manon,

Anastasia and Juliet as well as Katherina in *The Taming of the Shrew*. She also danced with Rudolf Nureyev in his fiftieth-birthday performance in Los Angeles.

In 1992, Alessandra scaled back her role at the ABT to become a guest star. The show she chose as her curtain call was, of course, *Romeo and Juliet*. She was appointed prima ballerina assoluta at La Scala in Milan.

Aged forty-four, Alessandra took what she believed to be her career's final bow, wanting to dedicate more time to her two daughters. She gave up not only ballet, but exercise, until she found she missed the creativity and fulfilment of dancing. After she started to suffer from joint pains, Alessandra started yoga and pilates again, then, gently, ballet classes. At the age of fifty-two she started to dance carefully picked roles professionally — not the high-octane, physically demanding parts she

once managed with ease, but those created for older dancers. She won huge acclaim for her triumphant and groundbreaking performances: the title role in *Duse*, Léa in *Chéri* (based on the novel by Colette) and, in another production that drew on literary inspiration, as Mrs Dalloway in the Royal Ballet's *Woolf Works*.

COLETTE

Danced the role of Léa in an adaptation of the novel *Chéri* written by

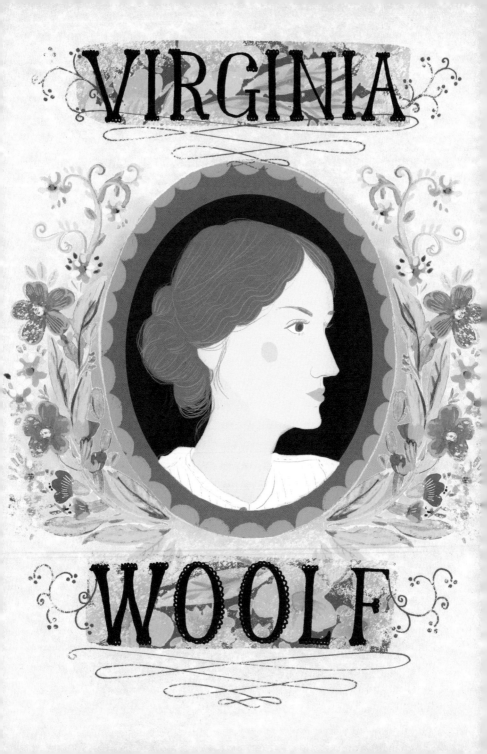

Orlando was turned into an opera with a libretto written by

GEORGE ELIOT

Wrote an essay in defence of

ANGELA CARTER

VIRGINIA WAS a complex, often tortured character, whose pioneering novels and writings still resonate deeply.

Adeline Virginia Stephen's father was a writer and mountaineer, and her mother a nurse and great beauty, immortalised in Pre-Raphaelite paintings. Virginia lived with them and her seven siblings and half-siblings in Kensington, London.

At first Virginia's early childhood was carefree, but sexual abuse by her half-brothers, and the deaths of her mother and her half-sister, led to several mental breakdowns. She didn't go to school, but trained in painting, then studied German, Greek and Latin at King's College, London. However, her father's death in 1904 completely derailed her, and she was briefly institutionalised.

The family sold their Kensington home and bought a townhouse in Bloomsbury, where they hosted weekly meetings of intellectuals, artists and free-thinkers: the Bloomsbury Group. Virginia met writer Leonard Woolf at the house, and the pair married in 1912.

Virginia had been writing reviews since 1905, as well as working on her novel, *Melymbrosia*. Twisted and compelling, it played with structure, narrative and dream-like prose, and in 1915 it was published as *The Voyage Out*. Two years later, the Woolfs established the experimental Hogarth Press and published several of Virginia's books, including *Mrs Dalloway*, *To the Lighthouse* and *The Waves*.

In 1922, Virginia met Vita Sackville-West, an aristocratic writer, and began an affair. Vita supported the mentally fragile Virginia, both emotionally and financially – Vita chose to publish her more commercial novels via Hogarth. In return, Virginia based the charming, eponymous hero of *Orlando* on Vita.

Established as a writer and public speaker, Virginia embarked on what was to be her final manuscript. As she wrote, she sank into deep depression. The Second World War was scorching Europe and Virginia was worried about what would happen to her and her Jewish husband if the Nazis invaded. When her house in London was bombed, Virginia could see no way out. She filled her coat pockets with stones and walked into the river near her second home in the Sussex countryside. Her body was found three weeks later.

Although Virginia Woolf and Georgia O'Keeffe never met, they were similar in their approach to their art. Both used flowers metaphorically – Virginia mentioned eighty different species in her fictional work alone, and one-sixth of Georgia's works were florally inspired. In May 1925, *The Dial* literary magazine used one of O'Keeffe's paintings, *Flagpole*, to illustrate a Woolf essay, 'The Lives of the Obscure'.

SINGLE-MINDED FROM an early age, Georgia's modern take on nature and landscape made her one of the most venerated artists of the twentieth century.

Growing up on a wheat farm in Wisconsin, Georgia was always connected to the land and nature. One of seven children, her interest in art was encouraged, and by ten she knew she would be an artist. She trained at the School of the Art Institute of Chicago and in New York, but had to move back to her family home in Charlottesville due to her father's bankruptcy, where she was forced to teach art.

In 1915, she was teaching at Columbia College when she started to experiment with charcoal abstracts, and before long her work was exhibited by photographer and promoter Alfred Stieglitz at the 291 gallery in New York. A year later, Georgia moved there and kindled a romantic and artistic relationship with Alfred – he took over 300 pictures of her, starkly beautiful – and they married in 1924. Initially, she began work on her trademark flower paintings, large-scale close-ups of perfect blooms, emotionally charged and intense. Then her pictures started to reflect her environment – she painted skyscrapers, capturing the exciting buzz of the Jazz Age in full swing. Georgia was now one of the most successful American artists.

Heartbroken following her husband's affair in 1928, Georgia escaped the city's suffocating social scene to New Mexico, where she bought a house, Ghost Ranch. She was inspired by the baked landscapes and bleached skulls, and the isolation suited her reclusive personality. In the

1940s, there were major solo exhibitions for Georgia, including at the Museum of Modern Art in New York, where she was the first woman to have a retrospective. In 1946, her still-beloved Alfred suffered a thrombosis, and she rushed to New York to be with him when he died. After settling his affairs, she moved permanently to New Mexico. She died at the age of ninety-eight, and her ashes were scattered around Ghost Ranch.

When she discovered Alfred's affair with young photographer Dorothy Norman, Georgia had a nervous breakdown and spent time in hospital. At her lowest ebb, she received a beautiful, supportive letter from her friend, the artist Frida Kahlo. Frida told her how worried she was about Georgia's sickness and how much she desired to see and speak to her again.

Attended the salons of Mabel Dodge Luhan, as did

GERTRUDE STEIN

The pair had first met in America in 1933, with Frida nurturing the friendship, perhaps hoping for something more romantic. Later, in 1951, Georgia was to return the support when she visited the bed-bound Frida in Mexico.

GEORGIA O'KEEFFE

Inspired a dress design by

ELSA SCHIAPARELLI

JOSEPHINE BAKER

While in Paris, she had an affair with

FRIDA KAHLO'S life story sang in acid-bright colours from her canvases. Iconic in the most literal of senses, she is famous as much for her bold look as for her incredible work and volatile, transgressive life.

Born Magdalena Carmen Frida Kahlo y Calderón in Mexico City, Frida was spirited and mischievous, despite a serious bout of polio at the age of six. She stood out at her school – not only was she one of few girls, but she dressed in brightly coloured traditional costumes. As a teen, she watched, riveted, for hours as the painter Diego Rivera sketched a mural on the school wall (to the annoyance of his then-wife Guadalupe 'Lupe' Marín). She and her schoolmates formed a rebellious, artistic gang, Los Cachuchas, many of whom went on to become Mexico's leading free-thinkers.

At the age of eighteen, Frida was involved in a bus accident, an event that left her suffering pain for the rest of her life. During her recovery, she started to paint. Many of her paintings were self-portraits; Frida made the ideal subject. She was unconventional — dressing as a boy, having affairs with women — and she looked spectacular.

In 1928, at twenty-one, Frida reconnected with Diego. He was forty-two, physically much bigger than Frida, but with a beta-male attitude that she loved – he went against the ingrained culture of the country and treated women as equals. The pair married in 1929 and led peripatetic lives as they travelled the world – Diego's commissions meant they went wherever he was painting.

Diego had numerous affairs, including with Frida's sister Cristina. Frida was hurt by Diego's womanising, and poured her emotions – heightened by several abortions and other operations – into her tiny, detailed works. It was almost like a painted diary. However, Frida did also have her own relationships with other men and women. She was rumoured to have had an affair with exiled Soviet communist Leon Trotsky who lived out some of his asylum at their house.

In 1939, following numerous liaisons on both sides, Diego divorced Frida. They remarried in 1940.

Frida, who declared herself to be a better artist than her husband, participated in exhibitions worldwide and painted the occasional portrait, but she wasn't truly acclaimed during her lifetime. However, after her death, due in part to her being heralded as a feminist trailblazer, the cult of Frida grew. Her paintings would go on to change hands for enormous sums.

The physically fragile Frida might not seem like the most likely subject for a ballet, but Annabelle Lopez Ochoa's *Broken Wings* tells the story of Frida and Diego. The piece, premiered at the English National Ballet in 2016, had as its star the ENB's dancer-director Tamara Rojo. Rojo had commissioned it as part of a triple bill of work by female choreographers – a highly unusual event in the industry.

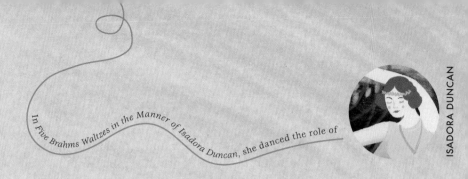

TAMARA ROJO'S ballet dreams didn't only encompass becoming a prima ballerina — she also wanted to have a wider, more creative impact on the world of classical dance.

The daughter of Spanish radical anti-Franco campaigners, Tamara was born in Canada, but the family moved back to Spain when she was four months old. Tamara's interest in dance was sparked when she saw her peers taking ballet classes after school in Madrid. She started training at five, becoming a full-time student at Madrid's Royal Conservatory of Dance at eleven. Her parents were incredibly supportive – making financial sacrifices to support Tamara – but also insisted that she attended academic evening classes. This dual education gave Tamara the intellectual and physical grounding necessary for her twin-pronged career.

Tamara left Madrid to join the Scottish National Ballet, performing principal roles before moving to the English National Ballet. There, Derek Deane created the role of Clara for her in his take on *The Nutcracker*, which was a critical and commercial success. She went on to the Royal Ballet, where she was made a principal dancer.

Tamara had a tendency at the time to push herself regardless of her physical condition: she danced Giselle with a sprained ankle and had her appendix burst during a performance. She was then re-hospitalised when she returned to the stage too early. However, in 2003, a serious foot injury made her appreciate that she needed to take more care of her body.

In 2006, the Spanish government approached Tamara about setting up a similar company to the ENB. The project didn't happen, but Tamara started thinking about working behind the scenes. She was mentored by Karen Kain at the National Ballet of Canada, then in 2012 became artistic director of the English National Ballet.

Tamara believes that dance is art, and communicates emotions, rather than pure athleticism, which she endeavours to transmit to her dancers. Her programming mixes the pragmatic – the company needs to be financially stable – with the daring. She has commissioned works by relatively obscure female choreographers, war-themed ballets and difficult pieces by William Forsythe and Pina Bausch.

Tamara said she was 'truly honoured and humbled' to present Pina's *The Rite Of Spring* in London, and paid tribute to Pina. 'Pina Bausch was an incredible artist, and remains one of the most influential people in modern culture today. Her work transcends description; it affects you on a deep emotional level, speaking to your spirit and defying logical analysis.'

was a fellow rebel against the ballet orthodoxy

PINA BAUSCH'S revolutionary creative methods caused a seismic shift in dance. Her focus on her performers' raw emotions, darkly dramatic sets and savage choreography sent shockwaves beyond the ballet world and into those of stage, film and TV.

Philippina (Pina) grew up in rooms above her parents' restaurant in Solingen. It was a place that formed her love of people-watching, as well being the perfect stage to hone her performing chops – she danced for guests. Her talent was evident, and at fourteen she started at Kurt Jooss's Folkwang Academy in Essen. His Tanztheater methods encouraged Pina to combine dance with drama, to mix established balletic rules with more freeform styles, and to absorb other arts and aim for holistic creativity.

Pina excelled, winning a scholarship to study at the Juilliard School in New York. She went on to perform with the Metropolitan Opera Ballet and New American Ballet. While in New York, she devoured high and low culture, strengthening her resolve to break down genre barriers.

Jooss lured her back to Essen to join his relaunched Folkwang Ballet, where she danced and helped Jooss choreograph, then produced her own pieces. In 1973, Pina became head of what would be known as Tanztheater Wuppertal, where she devised new genres to work in: dance operas and pieces using popular songs.

Pina's works were unapologetically dramatic: she went beyond conventional dance dogma and laid bare emotions. Her dancers challenged gender conventions, soared around surreal sets, and scoured themselves and their experiences for emotional resonance, all leavened with bursts of clownish humour. Her methods became hugely influential, and the company began to work with others around the world. Pina also collaborated with film directors, including Pedro Almodóvar and Wim Wenders, who would make a documentary about her life. Pina died of cancer just two days before filming on the documentary started.

Pina's 1977 *Bluebeard, Listening to a Tape Recording of Bela Bartok's Opera, 'Bluebeard's Castle'; A Piece by Pina Bausch* was first performed by Tanztheater Wuppertal. It was a wheels-within-wheels work inspired by the gothic folktale about a violent nobleman and serial wife-killer. Another artist moved by the tale was Angela Carter, who retold the story in an adult, grisly fashion as part of possibly her best-known work, *The Bloody Chamber*.

SPINNING FAIRY tales for grown-ups, Angela Carter brought a surreal, feminist perspective to what had previously been regarded as the most hackneyed of genres.

Born in wartime Eastbourne, Angela Carter's childhood was like its own nightmarish fairytale. Her journalist father and strait-laced mother were overprotective and overindulgent to the point of neuroticism. Angela was allowed to stay up past midnight, but wasn't allowed out of their sight – she had to wash with the bathroom door open even as a teenager. By seventeen she had rebelled. She shook off her parents' influence, started smoking and wearing short skirts and lost a lot of weight, a process that spiralled into anorexia.

Her parents wanted her to go to Oxford University, but Angela realised that they'd only come with her, so she rejected the idea. Instead, she followed her father into journalism, where she met industrial chemist and part-time record producer Paul Carter, with whom she went to folk shows and on CND marches. They married in 1960 – Angela seeing it as a way to escape her parents – and moved to Bristol, where she studied at the university. There she developed her own form of feminism, based around loosening up and subverting gender stereotypes.

Paul's subsequent depression isolated Angela, but she started publishing novels, receiving the Somerset Maugham Award for her third, *Several Perceptions*. She spent the prize money on a lone trip to Japan, where she met unsuitable boyfriends who thrilled and transformed her attitudes to gender relations. Her writing was starting to transform too — two books she published there showed a more ambitious scope. She divorced Paul by post.

After she left Japan, Angela became a writer-in-residence at a number of

universities including Sheffield, Brown, Adelaide and East Anglia, marrying again in 1977 and having a son. In 1979, she published her most famous work, a collection of short stories, *The Bloody Chamber*: reworkings of classic fairy tales including *Little Red Riding Hood*, *Puss in Boots* and *Bluebeard*. Her style suited the subject — her prose was thick with description and rich in fantasy, almost suffocatingly dense. Her heroines were assertive and full of transgressive desire: Red Riding Hood slept with the wolf while her grandmother's bones rattled under the bed.

During the 1980s, Angela started to gather acclaim, but it wasn't until after her death at fifty-one that the public came to love her work and her towering talent was appreciated.

Angela did not just write fiction — she was also a talented editor. Despite once referring to Leonora Carrington's work as

IRIS MURDOCH

once interviewed her heroine

'prim', Angela's 1986 collection *Wayward Girls and Wicked Women: An Anthology of Subversive Stories* included one of Leonora's. 'The Debutante' was a surreal story about a girl who frees a hyena from a zoo to take her place at her coming-out ball. The anthology gathered together tales that featured forthright, intelligent, multifaceted female characters, often with very bad manners – the kind of character that Angela was so adept at writing herself.

Carter

Had an affair with Max Ernst, as did

GALA DALÍ

Lived and worked alongside

KATI HORNA

LEONORA CARRINGTON'S dramatic life was front-loaded. By the time she'd reached twenty-five, she'd eloped with Max Ernst, met Salvador Dalí, escaped the Nazis, been given electric shock treatment and moved to Mexico.

Let's rewind a little. The Carringtons lived in a Gormenghast-like mansion in Lancashire called Crookhey Hall. A lone girl in a family of boys, Leonora lived a life surrounded by nature, with an Irish nanny who would tell her Celtic fairy tales. Expelled from two convent schools, Leonora was sent to Florence to learn to paint. On her return, she was presented at court, then indulged her blossoming love of surrealism at the Chelsea School of Art.

In 1937, Leonora met the forty-six-year-old German surrealist master Max Ernst at a party, and the pair fell in love. He left his wife, she ran away from home, and the two moved to France. There they were at the heart of the surrealist art movement, and Leonora started to create rich, symbolic works influenced by her beloved animals. The outbreak of the Second World War saw Max marked as a 'degenerate' by the Nazis, and he was interned by the French then rearrested by the Gestapo. He abandoned Leonora and fled to America with Peggy Guggenheim.

Leonora, broken, set her pet eagle free and escaped to Spain. She had a

breakdown and was hospitalised, given electroconvulsive therapy and put on heavy drugs. Her parents sent her nanny by submarine to rescue her from Madrid, but Leonora gave her the slip, finding a friendly face in Mexican poet Renato Leduc. He agreed to a marriage of convenience, and the pair moved firstly to New York, then subsequently to Mexico City, where a few years later Leonora would go on to marry Hungarian surrealist photographer Csizi Weisz and have two sons.

Her mythology-and-nature-soaked art and semi-autobiographical writing slowly became incredibly popular in Mexico. In the 1970s and 1980s, she was rediscovered and reappraised by academics and, as her death at the grand age of ninety-four approached, her paintings began to sell for large amounts of money.

Perhaps the happiest times of Leonora's life were alongside her close friends and fellow refugee artists Kati Horna and Remedios Varo. The trio met in Mexico and became coven-like close – their children even grew up together. In Remedios, Leonora found a fellow fan of spirits and the occult, and the pair gleefully studied alchemy, Tarot and astrology together. The two believed that women had rights to the 'mysteries' of magic powers handed down from ancient, pagan traditions.

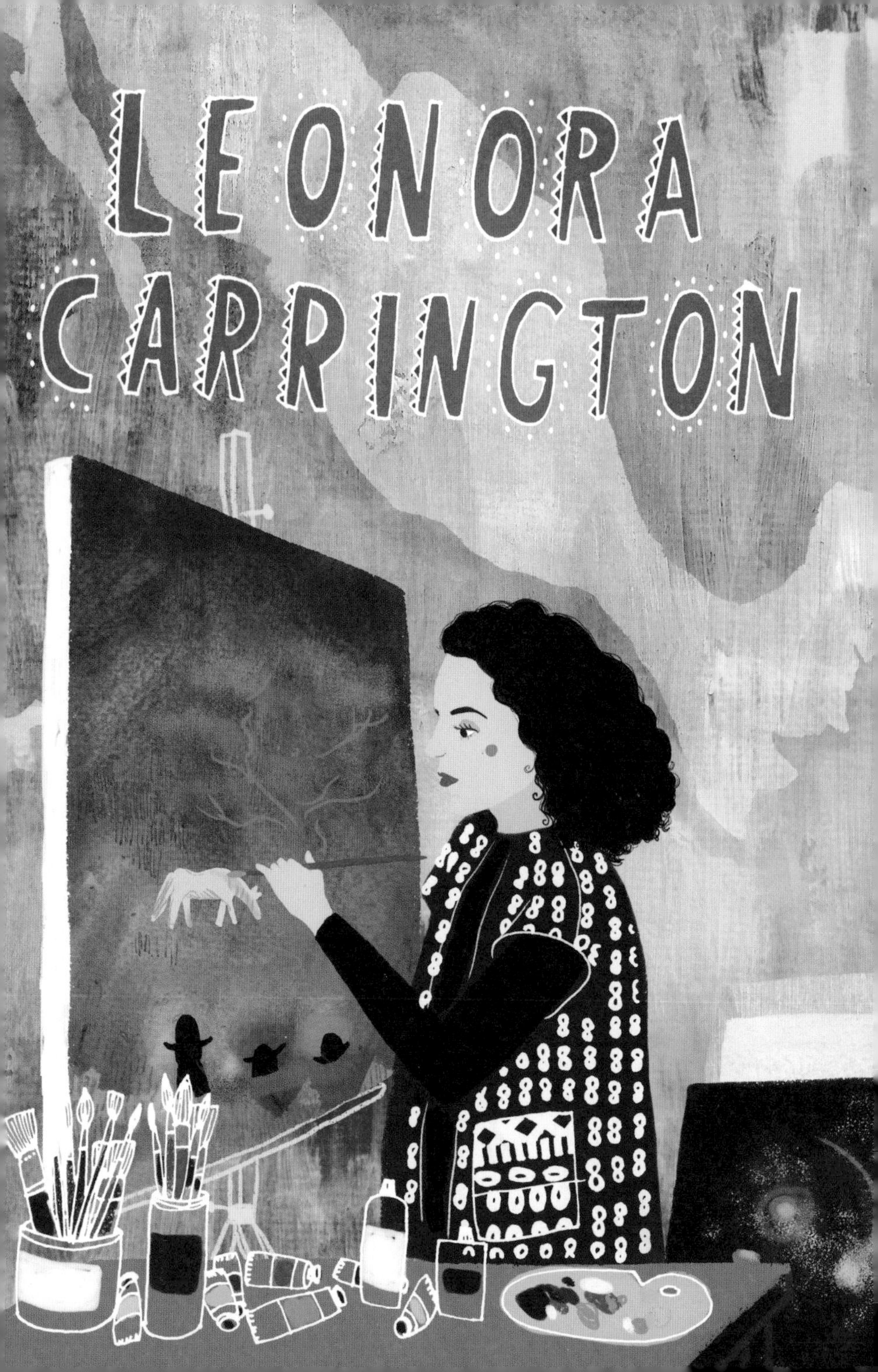
LEONORA
CARRINGTON

REMEDIOS VARO'S magic-infused, dream-like paintings were central to the Mexico City surrealist movement.

Remedios grew up in Girona, Spain. Her parents encouraged her artistic tendencies – her father was an engineer who taught her technical drawing – and the family's travels across the country and into North Africa meant Remedios was exposed to influences beyond her small-town upbringing. The family settled in Madrid, where Remedios attended school and the Real Academia de Bellas Artes de San Fernando. She started to become intrigued by surrealism, an

interest that was further fuelled by moves to Paris and then Barcelona during a short-lived first marriage.

In Barcelona, Remedios joined the Logicophobists collective, who aimed to tie together art and metaphysics in a way that defied logic and reason. Here she also met French surrealist poet Benjamin Péret, with whom she started a love affair. The two returned to Paris, where they became part of the surreal set, which included Leonora Carrington and André Breton, with whom she collaborated. However, Remedios felt that – perhaps due to her gender – she was not accorded the same

REMEDIOS VARO

artistic status as some of her peers. This feeling was later reflected in her work.

When the Nazis occupied France, Remedios was arrested for being a hated surrealist. On her release, she decided to flee to Mexico City, where she found kindred spirits in ex-pat artists and was inspired by the likes of locals such as Diego Rivera and Octavio Paz. To make ends meet, Remedios worked in commercial art and costume design. However, after she split from Péret, she fell in love with Walter Gruen, a rich Austrian businessman whose money allowed her to paint full-time.

Remedios' depictions of androgynous characters — sometimes performing scientific activities, sometimes in mystical settings, and sometimes representing the suppression of women in art — started to be exhibited and sold. Sadly, Remedios' career was cut short by her death from a heart attack at just fifty-five.

Remedios' magical world was captured in an earthy, more literal way by photographer Kati Horna, the third member of the surrealist trio. Kati took pictures of the three women's interwoven lives, providing an insight into their everyday world.

A SURREALIST photographer best known for her shots of the Spanish Civil War, Kati Horna's work was striking for both its aesthetic and politics.

Kati was born Kati Deutsch in Budapest, which at the time was in economic turmoil. As a teenager, she met legendary war photographer and superstar Robert Capa (then known as Endre Friedmann). Politically aware, they also used one another for their work. After Kati's father died, she decided that she'd earn her living taking pictures, also the perfect medium to communicate her radical views. Kati studied in Berlin, where she became part of a small group of activists that included theoretician Karl Korsch and playwright Bertolt Brecht, and started to figure out how she could combine politics, psychoanalysis and art.

Kati was reunited with Capa in Paris in the late 1930s, where she started to take picture series of flea markets and cafés, as well as experimenting with surrealism. She then followed Capa to Spain, where the Civil War was raging. While Capa had his lens focused on the action-packed battlefront, the more reserved Kati took compassionate, visionary pictures of those affected by war, capturing the resilience of women under siege.

Kati worked for anarchist titles such as *Umbral*, where she was graphic editor and where she met her husband-to-be, the artist José Horna. The couple escaped to Paris in 1939, then, during the Nazi occupation, travelled on to Mexico, where she established her close friendship with

Remedios Varo and Leonora Carrington. Kati had known Leonora's husband, 'Chiki' Weisz, as a girl in Hungary.

As well as having a daughter with José, Kati continued to take photos, many of them featuring masks and dolls and combining elements of the fantastical. She also produced portraits of the group of artists gathered in the city, including Alejandro Jodorowsky and Alfonso Reyes. Mexico City became Kati's muse — she took citizenship and shot her beloved adopted home for magazines.

'Inconsolable' after the death of Robert Capa in Vietnam, Kati's work matured further in the 1960s, which were considered to be the peak of her career. She shot more thoughtful stories, considering gender and transience, as well as architectural photographs. Teaching and working for magazines, she lived a long life, dying at the age of eighty-eight.

CLAUDE CAHUN

was a fellow pioneer of surrealist photography

KATI HORNA

Brimming with creative inspiration, how-to projects, and useful information to enrich your everyday life, quarto.com is a favourite destination for those pursuing their interests and passions.

First published in 2018 as *I Know a Woman*
by Aurum, an imprint of The Quarto Group
The Old Brewery, 6 Blundell Street
London N7 9BH
United Kingdom

www.Quarto.com

This edition first published in 2023 by White Lion Publishing

A catalogue record for this book is available from the British Library.

ISBN 978-0-7112-5587-6

10 9 8 7 6 5 4 3 2 1

Typeset in ITC Veljovic
Design by Paileen Currie
Cover design by Evelin Kasikov

Printed in China

MIX
Paper from
responsible sources
FSC® C016973

Acknowledgements
Dedicated to all the inspiring, supportive and hilarious women in my life: my mum Rhona, my daughter Dusty, Gloria and Jeannie, Esther, Guri, Sarah, Sarra, Hege, Nadia, Denise, Alix, Melissa, Mrs Kennedy, all Ye Nuns, Letty, Megan, Ingrid, Ann, Jane and Caroline. And the best men too: Jeff, Arthur, Tom and Colin. Huge thanks to: Sarah Papworth for her incredible illustrations, superstar agent Juliet Pickering and all at Blake Friedmann, Melissa Hookway at Aurum for her insight, encouragement and expertise, Josh Ireland for his sensitive, helpful editing, and Paileen Currie for her formidable design skills.